Pandanus Online Publications, found at the Pandanus Books
web site, presents additional material relating to this book.

www.pandanusbooks.com.au

The Hmong of Australia

The Hmong of Australia
Culture and Diaspora

Edited by
Nicholas Tapp and Gary Yia Lee

PANDANUS BOOKS
Research School of Pacific and Asian Studies
THE AUSTRALIAN NATIONAL UNIVERSITY

Cover: Hmong women selling vegetables at Salamanca market, Hobart, 1997.
Photography by Roberta Julian.

© Nicholas Tapp and Gary Yia Lee 2004

Typeset in Garamond 11pt on 13.5pt and printed by Pirion, Canberra

National Library of Australia Cataloguing-in-Publication entry

The Hmong of Australia.

        Bibliography.
        Includes index.
        ISBN 1 74076 041 7

        1. Hmong Australian — Social life and customs. 2. Hmong (Asian people) — Social aspects — Australia. 3. Hmong Australians — Cultural assimilation. I. Lee, Gary Y. (Gary Yia), 1951–. II. Tapp, Nicholas.

305.895942094

Editorial inquiries please contact Pandanus Books on 02 6125 3269

www.pandanusbooks.com.au

Published by Pandanus Books, Research School of Pacific and Asian Studies, The Australian National University, Canberra ACT 0200 Australia

Pandanus Books are distributed by UNIREPS, University of New South Wales, Sydney NSW 2052 Telephone 02 9664 0999 Fax 02 9664 5420

Production: Ian Templeman, Duncan Beard, Emily Brissenden

*This book is dedicated to the Hmong people of Australia
and to their better understanding.*

Contents

Introduction

Nicholas Tapp

In 2002 Gary Lee and I were fortunate enough to be given the chance, thanks to Francesca Merlan and other members of the Steering Committee, to organise a panel, 'Changing Cultural Contexts: Representations of the Hmong', at the Annual Meeting of the Australian Anthropological Society held at The Australian National University, Canberra (3–5 October). We believe this was the first time researchers on the Hmong in Australia had been enabled to come together to compare their findings in very different fields and to discuss a wide range of different issues concerning the Hmong population and society of Australia. Some seeding money came from a Chiang Ching Kuo Foundation for International Scholarly Exchange grant for a research project we held (see below), and our thanks are due to the Chiang Ching Kuo Foundation, in Taiwan, for this.

The Hmong, as Gary Lee's chapter explains, first arrived in Australia in 1975 from war-torn Laos, and many of the chapters here harken back to memories of that traumatic time. They have settled into Australia well as a small population of under 2,000, in Sydney, Melbourne, Hobart, and now also north Queensland and Brisbane and, as in other countries of resettlement such as France and the United States of America, their settlement has been characterised by the phenomenon of secondary migration to places other than those of their original settlement. Their early status as refugees was replaced by an innovative sponsorship programme under which those settled here were able to sponsor other close family relatives to settle in Australia. In Australia, as in other resettlement countries, the Hmong have been active in founding local and national associations to protect and safeguard their interests, and there is alarm about the rapid assimilation of the younger generation and their loss of traditional cultural heritage. The Australian Hmong is a small community, but a dynamic and rapidly changing one.

There have been many workshops and meetings on the Hmong in the United States where they number over 180,000,[1] in particular the Hmong-organised Hmong National Development conferences (see Julian's chapter in this volume), and two international research conferences organised in the early 1980s.[2] In China there have been several series of national and international meetings of provincial Miao Studies Associations which have included the Hmong together with other non-Hmong Miao people of China (like the Hmu, Kho Xiong and A Hmao) (see, *inter alia*, Schein 1996 and Tapp 2003). In 1998, the first International Hmong/Miao Studies Conference was organised by Jean Michaud and Christian Culas in Aix-en-Provence, France (CNRS, 11–13 September), and the proceedings of this are shortly to be published (Tapp, Michaud, Culas, and Lee, eds, forthcoming). There were plans to hold a second conference, in Australia or Thailand, which have not yet materialised.

From an anthropological point of view the Canberra conference panel was significant in focusing on a topic which has so far not been a particular province of anthropologists in Australia, immigrant communities to Australia itself.[3] Although significant and substantial work has certainly take place on these populations (see, for example, De Lepervanche 1984, Craig 1965, Martin 1978, Bottomley 1992, Inglis 1992 and Thomas 1999), in general S.F. Nadel's vision of a union of sociology with anthropology in Australia has not taken place and the main concern of anthropologists here seems to have focused on indigenous communities (in the strictest definition of that word) and those overseas, particularly among Australia's neighbours in Asia and the Pacific. As Bottomley (1998) observed, until now 'anthropologists have demonstrated relatively little interest in the massive immigrations to Australia and the marked heterogeneity of the population'. We had hoped that by organising such a panel at this particular conference, we might open a way for others to take up more intensive studies of immigrant communities in Australia from the theoretical viewpoint of a contemporary anthropology.

However, contributions came from a wide range of academic disciplines, including music (ethnomusicology), anthropology, sociology, medicine, linguistics and museology. It is certainly the case that the lines between anthropology, history, and geography on the one hand, and anthropology, cultural studies, English literature, and sociology on the other, are running particularly thin at the moment, and it was a tribute to the organisers of this conference that they were able to welcome papers from such a wide range of disciplines.

It must be said that the contributors to this volume represent virtually all the serious researchers who have devoted their attentions to the Hmong in Australia. While encouraged by such work and the rich diversity of backgrounds and interests it represents, nevertheless the paucity of such research to date (and particularly, I may add, the lack of significant research by younger Australian Hmong themselves) on such a significant minority population in the country was somewhat disappointing.

This lack of academic research on the Hmong has been more than compensated for by the plethora of studies of another kind of the Hmong; these have been mostly government-sponsored or local community surveys of population, health, housing, medicine, diet, childbirth, employment, and so on. This has led to a very real 'research fatigue' among the Hmong living in Australia, most of whom are busy citizens with lives and careers to get on with who do not see why they should necessarily be targeted as the objects of other peoples' studies and career trajectories, and where they expect quite legitimately to be told what the purpose of such research is and what tangible benefits they may expect to receive from it.

The panel itself was exciting and interesting I think for all of us, working in separate fields with few opportunities hitherto to meet others with similar interests and research experiences; we all learned from each other and exchanged ideas in a fruitful and candid way. For me the moral of the meeting came in the masterly summing up by Dr Gary Lee. Almost all of us, in our various papers and presentations, and in the discussions following those presentations (which were unfortunately not recorded), had been concentrating on the distinctive 'Hmong-ness' of the Hmong, the difficulties of their adjustment to a new society in Australia, their attempts to find new ways of 'being Hmong', and so on. Indeed, in conversations with the Hmong who were not brought up in Australia, it is often difficult to avoid this sort of tenor in general discussions of Hmong issues; very frequently conversations gravitate towards an appreciation of the importance and unique distinction of Hmong traditional customs (*kevcai*) and culture (a view I strongly uphold), fears and regrets at their impending loss by the younger generation, and a variety of practical suggestions for how to maintain and continue Hmong traditional customs (including an idea to send young Australian Hmong teenagers to Asia to teach English to Asian Hmong, and learn Hmong customs and language in return).[4] But in Gary Lee's summary, he pointed out how many of the papers, and how much of our discussion, had focused on the importance of being Hmong in a strange and alien setting. 'But a lot of us', he said in his dry, Australian way (we were talking English), 'have been trying very hard to be Australian!' And *not* being accepted as such, he went on to emphasise, referring to how he felt his soul was Australian, but his face was Hmong, or Asian, so people here inevitably related to him as an Asian and a foreigner. This was a salutary reminder to many of us of the ethnic prejudice and innuendos, the difficulties and lack of understanding, that many Hmong, like other Asian immigrants here, face every day in their struggle to be accepted as full members of society.

The following chapters are based on presentations made at that conference, except that Pranee Rice withdrew her paper on Hmong courtship and marriage in Melbourne and submitted one on menstruation instead. All have been more than fully revised and edited for publication.

Gary Lee's chapter reflects the experience he has gained, since his first arrival in Australia as a schoolboy under the Colombo Plan in

1965, in dealing with community and refugee or immigrant problems of the Hmong, and the deep knowledge he has accumulated of the Hmong in all their global homes. Factual and unemotional in tone, the chapter provides a masterly overview of the current situation of the Hmong from a sociological viewpoint. Dealing with issues of early settlement, housing and employment, and secondary migration, the chapter also describes the establishment of associations by the Hmong and confronts issues of cultural continuity and adaptation which passionately concern all Hmong.

My own chapter represents some of the findings of a Chiang Ching Kuo Research Project, 'Communal Voluntary Diasporic Public Cultures: Hmong Transnationalism in Asia and Overseas', undertaken with Gary Lee, for which research was carried out among Hmong communities in China, Thailand, Laos, Taiwan and Australia. To a large extent it represents work in progress since it is still planned to extend this project to Vietnam, France, Canada, the United States and other overseas sites of the Hmong, while those already visited require further and deeper research. Nevertheless, the concerns in this chapter with the Hmong as a diasporic community and the changes this is bringing about for the Hmong social structure and sense of identity are echoed in most of the other chapters, particularly those of Roberta Julian and Maria Wronska-Friend.

Roberta Julian's chapter is an example of the kind of work which I feel there should be much more of; based on many years of experience with the Hmong and other migrant communities in Tasmania, and a familiarity with the situation of the Hmong in America, she combines approaches from sociology and anthropology, literary and cultural analysis, together with an historical outlook, to piece together a vision of the Hmong as a community not only in Australia, but also in the world. This chapter is shot through with sophisticated theoretical insights presented in a clear and compelling way, particularly on the varying levels of Hmong Tasmanian identity in Australia, and on the likely effects of globalisation at the local and national levels.

Maria Wronska-Friend's chapter adds to this vision of a diasporic, far-flung community nevertheless firmly located and situated in Australia, by presenting the results of her extensive work with and knowledge of the Hmong community of north Queensland. Her research has been an active and participatory one since she has been instrumental in organising a number of exhibitions and events connected with the Hmong community. By focusing in detail on changes in the traditional Hmong costume, and the new meanings it has gathered in the Australian context, she also shows us how contemporary image and the cultural heritages of history intersect for the Australian Hmong. And by examining the provenance of particular items of clothing she succeeds in providing a fascinating account of how these articles of material culture express and embody the close familial relationships which are today located in disparate and widely separated quarters of the world.

More importantly for the future of the Hmong, the combined use of varied costumes from different parts of the world and different Hmong sub-groups points to a more generalised postmodern Hmong group image, reflecting a truly global Hmong identity.

Catherine Falk's masterly study of Hmong music as expressed through the *qeej* reed-pipe instrument also shows us this instrument as an icon of contemporary as well as historical cultural identity and points to its current dissemination globally on the internet. Yet this chapter reflects more deeply on the relationship between musical and social forms generally, and provides an historical account of the reception and development of the instrument in changing cultural contexts, based on intensive textual and ethnographic research, which is of great value. Her suggestions as to the very great antiquity of this instrument in the Chinese records are extremely interesting and may point towards an early shamanic use of this famous instrument in China.

Pranee Rice Liamputtong's chapter reflects but one aspect of her wider and far more extensive work on the health and traditional medicinal system of the Hmong community in Australia (see Liamputtong 2000). The interest in Hmong medicine and health has of course been a general one, particularly in the United States where a number of books now testify to the strength of this system and the shock of its encounter with Western biomedicine (such as Fadiman 1997). Here we hear Hmong women talking frankly to other women about highly personal issues in a way which alerts us to the significance of other systems of belief and medical approaches. This chapter also reflects aspects of the wider interest in issues of gender among the Hmong which has been approached by several writers and is a growing field of study.[5]

Finally, Nerida Jarkey's chapter deals with what is perhaps at the heart of all anthropological inquiry: do people of different languages and different cultural backgrounds have radically dissimilar ways of understanding the world? Raising the question of cultural relativism in its most extreme form, the chapter focuses on a particular detail of Hmong linguistic structure in order to show that, in this instance at least, no radically disparate world-view is involved. The chapter will be of interest not only to comparative linguists, but also for showing how general scientific theory and understanding depends on the use of concrete ethnographic example, in this case taken from the rich field of the Hmong language.

The authors hope this book may serve to give a general reader some idea of the wide range of issues which research on the Hmong in Australia has covered, as well as a basic introduction to this fascinating and not well enough known community. We also hope the book will be of interest to members of the Hmong community in understanding why they are so frequently the objects of fascinated research attention. In many ways the book is a tribute to the richness and importance of the cultural system the Hmong of today have inherited, and we think that interest will be shared, and appreciated, by most members of the Hmong community. In other ways more abstract issues to do with the effects of globalisation on local communities, social changes and the relationship of minority groups to the state, are also being addressed in these pages through the use of Hmong examples, and we hope this collection may also make those more general interests more comprehensible to average members of the Hmong community. Beyond Australia the book should be of interest not only to those who work on, or with, the

Hmong in many other countries, but should also contribute to general understandings of processes of social change among recent immigrants to new countries of settlement, the relations they may hold with homelands and the new relations forged with other diasporic communities overseas.

Finally, both editors and contributors would like to express our sense of deep gratitude to members of the Hmong community in Australia, who have helped all of us in various ways with our research projects. Without their assistance, none of this work would have been possible and we thank them for their time and patience in answering what at times must seem very repetitive and meaningless, if not intrusive, questions. We hope that in some way the results of this research feed back to that community in the form of an increased general understanding of what it means to be Hmong in an Australian setting, and perhaps also an appreciation of how hard it may be for those of the Hmong who have also been struggling, as Gary Lee's summary at the Conference so well put it, to be accepted as Australians.

Note on Orthography and Usage

Throughout this book, we have adopted the standard Romanised Phonetic Alphabet (RPA) system of orthography for Hmong developed by Bertrais, Heimbach, and Smalley (see Heimbach 1979). In this system, the final consonants indicate one of the eight Hmong tones, and so should not be pronounced as consonants at all, while a doubled vowel indicates final nasalisation. Thus, 'Hmong' is spelt 'Hmoob', the -b ending indicating a high level tone, and the 'oo' pronounced as 'ong'. There are no final endings to syllables outwith final nasalisation, otherwise this system would not work. The only other real peculiarity of the system is that 'x' is pronounced exactly like the English 's', while 's' is pronounced something like the English 'sh'. I understand this peculiarity was the result of incompatibilities between the system developed by the Roman Catholic, and that developed by the Protestant, missionaries who worked with the Hmong at that time. A preliminary 'h' indicates initial aspiration, through the nose.

Between the two main cultural divisions of the Hmong outside China, the Hmoob Dawb (White Hmong) and Hmoob Ntsuab (Green Hmong), RPA was developed mainly for the dialect spoken by the White Hmong, which displays systematic variations from the Green Hmong dialect (for example, of tone). In fact the Green Hmong pronunciation of this term for themselves is not pre-aspirated, and so should really be spelt 'Moob' or (in ordinary English approximation) 'Mong', and recently the American Green Hmong have begun a campaign arguing for the name to be changed to accord with their own usage; thus, they would prefer to be referred to as 'Mong', and not 'Hmong'. While this is a perfectly reasonable point, we have retained the normal spelling of 'Hmong' here because it is so generally known and accepted, and it would be confusing to general readers to do otherwise. It may be that at some point in the future, the Hmong community as a whole will decide to change the spelling of their name, or will agree to be known under two separate names, and if that time comes we should of course follow the usage which has been agreed on. At the moment, however, there is no such agreement, and so we have retained the more traditional usage.

'Ntsuab' itself is a colour term which refers to a tone midway between 'Green' and 'Blue' in English. In some earlier works (for example, Geddes 1976 or Nusit 1976) the Hmoob Ntsuab were referred to as the 'Blue Hmong'. However, the shade is closer to 'Green' and 'Green' is the more correct translation of this term, and is therefore the one which has been adopted here. It should be added that there is now some dissension about even this term, since some of the Green Hmong in the United States have recently objected to the use of this term, which they find is derogatory, and prefer to be called 'Moob Lees' (Mong Leng) instead. This is in fact historically incorrect; while the Hmong from Laos tend to think that 'Hmoob Ntsuab' and 'Hmoob Lees' are interchangeable terms for the same group of people, in fact the Hmoob Lees are, or were, a distinct group who seem to have become assimilated to the Hmoob Ntsuab in Laos and Thailand but remain distinct in Vietnam today.[6]

Footnotes

[1] The 2000 US Census gives a figure of 169,482 for those identifying only as Hmong, 186,310 for those who identified as Hmong as well as another ethnic group.

[2] The Second Hmong Research Conference ('The Hmong in Transition') was held at the University of Minnesota on 17–19 November 1983; the First in 1982 ('The Hmong in the West').

[3] A notable recent exception would be the work of Thomas (1999).

[4] The problems here would probably be the reluctance of most Australian Hmong teenagers to go to Asia at all (see Tapp, this volume), together with the dangers of life in Asia for them, particularly regarding their personal security and health (Gary Lee, personal communication).

[5] See, for example, Donnelly (1994) and Symonds (2003), besides a growing number of contributions by younger Hmong women.

[6] See Lemoine (1995); Hmoob Lees or 'Multicoloured Hmong' are known as Meo Hoa in Vietnamese, the Hmoob Ntsuab or 'Green Hmong' as Meo Xanh.

Culture and Settlement
The Present Situation of the Hmong in Australia

Gary Yia Lee

Introduction

It has been nearly thirty years since the first Hmong families arrived to settle in Australia in March 1976. Many more families followed until 1992 when the last were accepted from refugee camps in Thailand. Today, they number about 1,800.

Given that most of them were former soldiers or subsistence farmers from Laos, how have they managed with their new life in highly industrialised urban Australia? This chapter will try to shed some light on this question and update the current state of Hmong settlement in the country since the first overview on the subject which I gave at an international conference on Hmong refugees in 1983 (Lee 1986).

Settlement

The Hmong form part of the Indochinese refugee intake that the Australian government took from the newly installed communist regimes in Vietnam, Cambodia and Laos in 1975. Technically, they are Lao refugees of Hmong ethnicity. At the beginning, it was relatively easy to get accepted into Australia under the United Nations Convention, so many refugees stayed for only a short time in the camps along the Thai border with Laos. Then there were only simple forms to fill in, but these bureaucratic requirements gradually became more complicated as forms become more formalised and longer. When the never-ending stream of applicants became larger, it was more difficult for Indochinese asylum seekers to be recognised as genuine refugees by the United Nations High Commissioner for Refugees (UNHCR) and Australia. Some were seen as economic rather than political refugees. During the 1980s, many Hmong families were thus accepted under the Family Reunion programme rather than as political refugees. Under this programme, relatives already living in Australia had to submit sponsorship applications for those left behind in Thai refugee camps. The latter were then interviewed by Australian immigration officials to see if they were suitable for settlement in Australia. If they were accepted, they then underwent medical checks and waited in the Phanat Nikhom transit centre in Chonburi from three to six months for their departure.

Once arrived in Australia, most Hmong refugees chose to live where their sponsoring relatives were already established, mostly in the main cities of the eastern states. By 1984, the Hmong numbered 81 families with 384 persons found in Sydney (215 persons), Melbourne (112), Hobart (37), Adelaide (11) and Canberra (9). The population was relatively young with 55 per cent under the age of eighteen (Lee 1988: 535).

By 1996, the Australian census revealed a total of 1,420 Hmong speakers in Australia dispersed in the following way: 603 in Queensland, 384 in Victoria, 272 in Tasmania, 126 in New South Wales, 29 in the Australian Capital Territory, seven in Western Australia and five in South Australia. Compared to the 1984 population figures, the Hmong have become more numerous through further intakes from Thailand and natural increase, although they have remained one of the smallest ethnic communities in Australia. Queensland has become the state with the largest number of Hmong, due to secondary migration from the southern states to Cairns and Innisfail. By 1992, intakes of Hmong refugees from Thai camps had virtually ceased with the planned closing of all the refugee camps in Thailand that year by the UNHCR and the Thai authorities. Thus, any demographic changes within the Hmong community in Australia are due to internal population movements, and any increase in the number of Hmong in Queensland means a decrease in other states, particularly in New South Wales.

The first Queensland migration occurred in 1987 when Mr Lao Lee and his family from Sydney started a banana farm in Innisfail and attracted a lot of interest from other Hmong (see also Tapp, this volume). The family was reported to make good money working for itself, compared to the majority of other Hmong who continued to work in unskilled jobs bringing in only small wages. After 1993, other families had decided to sell their family homes and move to Innisfail. Gradually, they were joined by other families from Melbourne and Hobart. The reason for most of them was to go into the banana growing business, with more than twenty families buying banana plantations. Other families migrated to be with relatives, or to live in a tropical environment with vegetation that reminded them of their old mountain life in Laos, unlike other parts of Australia with their monotonous boring gum trees. Those without banana farms themselves often found work with those who had such farms. Others settled in Cairns where they work in hotels and restaurants as cooks and dish-washers, or as vegetable-stall keepers.[1]

Apart from this internal migration, the Hmong community in Australia has also experienced change due to some men marrying Hmong wives from Laos, France or the United States. A few young women have also joined their Hmong husbands living in the United States or France. So far three young men and about ten young women have made such a move. Some met their spouses through the internet, others through visits to relatives in the United States or in Australia. By and large, however, this inter-country migration has been small, except for a group of fifteen Hmong families with about 80 persons who were accepted by New Zealand in 1998, but have since all crossed the Tasman Sea to live with the larger Hmong population of Australia.

In mid-2003, it was estimated that there were 104 Hmong families living in far north Queensland (Cairns, Innisfail and Atherton) with more than 800 members. Sydney has 28 families and 140 persons, Canberra seven families with 30 persons, Melbourne more than 70 families and 435 persons, Hobart thirteen families and 95 persons, and Adelaide one family with four people (a Hmong man married to an Australian wife). The 1996 Australian census shows a Hmong family with six persons living in Perth, but not much is known about them as no contact has been possible. The latest trend for the Hmong is secondary migration towards Brisbane where there are more than 60 families and close to 350 persons. The current population number of more than 1,700 Hmong living in Australia has not changed much since 1996. There have been about 40 deaths since 1976, and natural increase has been small as young Hmong couples gradually adopt the Australian habit of having fewer children. The average Hmong couple now tends to have about four children, compared to their parents who may have had from six to eight surviving children a generation ago.

Before 1994 there were no Hmong living in Brisbane, but cheaper housing and a warmer climate began to attract many of those living in the southern states, particularly those from New South Wales and Victoria where by 2003 house prices had become so high that many young families could no longer afford to buy their own homes. Some of those who moved more recently were able to buy houses built on five-acre land parcels that could still be obtained for around $200,000 when such a sum would not even buy a small building block of 600 square metres in the southern states. Chambers Flat, a semi-rural suburb in southern Brisbane, now has many Hmong families living in this way. Other families bought homes in other nearby suburbs, although they live quite dispersed from one another, unlike the Hmong in other cities who tend to live in close proximity to each other. The reason for this wide dispersal may be due to the fact that different families moved to Brisbane at different times and from different states, not always knowing each other well so that there was less reason to stay close together. They are also the latest of a migration trend, having lived in other states for a long time and so are now able to look after themselves well. They thus do not feel the need to live near other Hmong, although there is still much interaction between them.

Occupations and Social Mobility

As with most refugees, the Hmong are predominantly political asylum seekers who were accepted into Australia on this basis or on the grounds of family reunion. This means that education and qualifications were not at the top of the criteria for their admission into the country, although the Australian government was selective in regard to a preference for younger people and smaller families. In Sydney in 1987, for example, only twelve of the 80 Hmong families there had members who were older than 50, mainly elderly parents living with their married children. In 1995, it was found that of the 32 Hmong households remaining in Sydney, 37 per cent of their members were in the 0–10 age group, with 54 per cent under twenty (Wang 1998–99: 40). The Hmong population was thus relatively young, compared to the Australian average of 54.3 per cent under 35 years of age, according to the 1991 census.

Laos was not only one of the least developed countries in Southeast Asia, with few schools and road infrastructures that allowed access between cities and country residences, but also had been ravaged by civil war on and off since 1953. The Hmong who lived in rural and remote areas of the country had few opportunities to study in the lowlands where most schools were. More schools were built in Hmong settlements after the 1970s, so that nearly all the younger Hmong who arrived in Australia before 1985 had received at least some primary schooling in Laos, with a few even having completed high school or teacher training college. Most of their parents were, however, illiterate, although some went on to study English in Australia and managed to achieve some literacy. With their subsistence farming background and lack of formal education, many of the older Hmong were eager to take up English lessons as a first step towards settling into the Australian community. In those days, the Australian government was still generous with migrant and refugee services with no restrictions on the number of hours one spent learning English. Many older Hmong were able to study English for a few years, rather than the 530 hours allocated to new migrants today.

During the early years of their arrival here, it was relatively easy for the Hmong to get factory jobs if they were willing to do any kind of work. Employers were mainly interested in workers who were prepared to learn and to work hard. There was also less competition for jobs, since there were few or no written or general knowledge tests of the type to which today's employers usually subject job applicants. Many Hmong, both men and women, were thus able to obtain paid work within three to six months of entering Australia. They were keen to leave the migrant hostels to settle in the general community, and wanted to work in order to achieve this. Although some sought jobs through the then Commonwealth Employment Service, the majority found work through friends and relatives, or private employment agencies.

Apart from a few months spent studying English, hardly anyone took up re-training to return to their former professions such as teaching or the public service. Most did not have tertiary education, unlike Vietnamese refugees, some of whom were able to re-enter their old fields of work. The Hmong realised too well that they could not compete against native English speakers, nor did they have the time to undertake long courses of studies. Family obligations and the need to re-establish themselves as quickly as possible in their new country meant that the sooner they could become self-supporting, the better it would be for their families. Young children became the priority for parents who, like all migrants, pinned their hopes more realistically on the next generation rather than themselves.

Nevertheless, the employment rate of the Hmong in general has continued to improve over the years. In 1987, for example, 35 per cent of the Hmong community in Sydney were unemployed and of those employed, 93 per cent were process workers doing unskilled factory jobs (Lee 1987). In 1995, Wang (1998–99: 48) discovered that this unemployment rate had come down to 27 per cent (12.5 per cent among females and 33 per cent among males) with a significant proportion of those employed doing semi-skilled or unskilled jobs, compared to 93 per cent in 1987. The number of skilled workers had also increased (30 per cent among females and 19 per cent among males). The few who could obtain formal qualifications seemed to be in more secure and well paid jobs — a trend that, Wang (1998–99: 49) observes, may continue for those younger Hmong who are still at school today.

During their first years in Australia, the main tangible sign of the Hmong's ability to adapt and move ahead was the possession of cars, at least one for each family. Cars were seen not only as a symbol of wealth, but an essential means for getting to work, for shopping or to socialise. Soon, however, a few Hmong families began to buy their first homes. By the mid-eighties, many of them were living in houses that they had bought or were paying off. Wang (1998–99: 42) found that 42 per cent of the 32 families she surveyed in Sydney already owned their own homes by 1995 and 19 per cent were paying them off. This represents a much higher rate of home ownership than the Australian average of 41 per cent, and far higher than the figures of 13 per cent for Vietnamese and 14 per cent for Cambodian-born refugees. Wang attributes this to the fact that the Hmong prefer to direct their money into more productive use by paying off their mortgages rather than spending it on rental accommodation. Hmong families also help each other with deposits towards the purchase of houses for relatives, thus allowing more of them to own their homes much earlier.

Apart from their own principal place of residence, a number of Hmong families have also gone into real estate investment — with six families now having from one to five investment properties. This high rate of home ownership has enabled many Hmong families to migrate later to Cairns and Innisfail in north Queensland, as mentioned above, using the money they obtained from the sale of their houses to buy farm lands or to finance their move, to purchase new houses, and to lease or buy their banana farms or other businesses. Many of those who did not have this initial capital have also worked hard hiring out their labour in banana plantations, or doing market gardening. This has allowed some to buy their own houses, while others still remain in rented accommodation.

Having been in Australia for thirty years with only a small population and the second generation just starting to get into the work force, the Hmong may not have made much headway into various social and economic strata of the Australian community. However, most have been able to re-establish themselves economically, found employment and become homeowners — even those who have not been able to find permanent employment. Given their background as subsistence farmers, students and soldiers in Laos, they have done well in the face of many language, social and cultural barriers.

The Community

On the whole, the majority of the older Hmong in Australia tend to stay among themselves and have little or no social interaction with people outside their own small community. In a sense, this is no different from most ethnic groups. The first generation of new arrivals often maintains some strong community ties that continue to hold them together as a linguistic and cultural community, while the second generation of children who are born or raised in the new country tends to venture further into the broader community and prefers to mix socially with other groups.

The Hmong are no different in this adjustment pattern. Like other communities, they have learned to adopt various means to help them settle into their new life in a Western and predominantly Christian society. Their traditional social structure of clans and extended families has been disrupted by the long years of war and resettlement as refugees in various parts of the world. No one family has been able to have all its relatives living in one country: there may be a few closely related married brothers together in Australia, but married sisters may have gone to America or France with their husbands, while other relatives may still be left behind in Laos. The Hmong have thus gone through a real global diaspora, and with it many adjustments have had to be made to their cultural practices and traditional social relations.

Among these changes, the most important are those relating to the clan system, used as the primary means of identifying relationships on the basis of the sharing of a clan name, whom one could marry and whom one could not marry, and who could participate in a family's ritual performances, funerals and celebrations. In the first ten years of their settlement, only eight clans were represented among the Hmong in Australia: Chang, Lee, Moua, Thao, Vang, Vue, Yang and Xiong. Later, members of the Hang and Kue clans were added. But this still does not include all sixteen clans as is commonly found in Southeast Asia. This has somewhat restricted the choice of marriage partners since Hmong can only marry outside their own clan group. In a sense, however, this situation has also forced the Hmong to forge other ties in order to remain close as a community on grounds other than by clan relationship alone.

A new social structure that the Hmong have adopted as an additional means to help in their settlement is the formation of mutual assistance associations. The first such organisation was the Hmong Australia Society (HAS) which was formed by Dr Pao Saykao in Melbourne in 1978.

The Society aims to unite all Hmong residents in Australia as a community in order to maintain the Hmong identity. It serves as the focus where the Hmong turn for assistance in times of need, sickness and bereavement. It also promotes understanding of the Hmong and their culture to the broader Australian society. The Society has a federal body and is represented in different states by state branches with executive committees. The federal executive committee rotates every two years between Tasmania, Victoria, New South Wales and Queensland where most of the Hmong live. Nearly all Hmong in Australia were HAS members.

In the early years, HAS initiated many projects for members, such as teaching Hmong language and culture to Hmong school children, and provided settlement information sessions on various subjects deemed useful for the successful integration of the Hmong into the Australian community. It held social functions, picnics and the Hmong New Year celebration to encourage members to get together as often as possible. In order to promote Hmong culture, classes on Hmong religious rituals were also held for interested young adults to learn to perform rituals in their own homes. HAS also participated in festivals and celebrations organised by local councils and other groups by lending them Hmong costumes and handicrafts for display, or giving talks and traditional dance performances. Young Hmong dancers became very popular and were often invited to perform in various locations in each state. Within the Hmong community, HAS executive members were kept busy helping with family problems, collecting members' contributions towards funeral costs, and ensuring that members followed the Society's rules regarding funeral arrangements, wedding costs and dowries.

In later years, many of these activities stopped as HAS members became more skilled in finding their own way around the broader community. Hmong language learning through formal classes also ceased, as young children grew up preferring to speak English. Disagreements among members in Victoria and far north Queensland also saw some members splitting away from HAS and forming their own small associations such as the Hmong Federation Council. A need-specific group, the SPK Inc., also came into existence in Cairns to serve the housing needs of new Hmong arrivals in the area. These new groups, and other factors, have now made many of the HAS activities redundant. There have been talks about abolishing HAS, but the majority of members want to keep it going for, if nothing else, it still retains its major function of collecting member contributions for funerals and other emergencies.

One of the original aims of HAS which brought high hopes and great enthusiasm to members in the early years was the teaching of religious rituals and cultural performances for younger members. Although many sessions were held using elderly ritual experts and experienced funeral reed-pipe players as teachers, the programme only ran for a year and yielded few results. The few young men interested in such cultural learning were also too busy working for a living and found the extra time they had to put in during evenings or weekends too demanding. Similar classes are now being held in Melbourne with good participation, and it is hoped that they will be more successful. A few ritual experts were later sponsored from the refugee camps to come and help with the community's spiritual needs, but their small number did not amount to much in terms of promoting and maintaining the community's cultural knowledge.

The Next Generation

Having been in Australia for nearly thirty years, one of the biggest challenges to the Hmong is the loss of traditions and language among the younger members of the community. Like other migrant groups, members of the younger generation quickly learn to adopt social values and behaviour patterns considered to be alien or detrimental to the beliefs and culture of their parents. Up to the age of six, most children speak Hmong well and are not shy to do so. As soon as they start going to school, however, they gradually come to use more and more English so that by the time they reach puberty few want to speak Hmong or even know how to anymore.

Few also take part or show much interest in religious rituals as they are observed or performed by their parents. The Hmong practices of animism and ancestor worship mean that a family head has to know how to carry out at least some simple rituals, for the Hmong's religion is essentially a family religion. Many elderly Hmong today are concerned that their traditional religious practices will die out after they are gone, and no one will know how to make offerings to them in the afterworld.

Even with the present first generation, this process of cultural and religious degeneration is already occurring with some husbands knowing less about rituals than their wives. Although women can also perform household rituals, the latter are generally men's responsibility. Men who have formal education spent many years away from their families to gain this education, and are thus less skilled in ritual matters. However, their wives are often more familiar with preparing ritual food and may know more about performing small household rituals. They are thus the cultural carriers in such households. Apart from this, it has been found that children who grew up in Australia but who were born overseas are usually more accepting of their parents' religious practices and associated food offerings to ancestors. They will at least eat ritual food which is often prepared from chicken or small pigs slaughtered for the purpose. Children who are born in Australia and who are not familiar with such practices often shun the consumption of such food, let alone take an active interest in the rituals themselves.

Another challenge to the Hmong in Australia is the difference between the expectations of parents of their children's academic achievements, and the actual outcomes. As stated above, the majority of parents did not have a high school education, but were willing to work hard in order to put their children through the education system at as high a level as possible. They put all their hopes for good jobs and high pay in their children, and have high expectations of the latter achieving these hopes. However, few Hmong children in Australia have been able to fulfill their parents' academic expectations. Many are more eager to get into the work force, even if it means doing unskilled menial jobs, than trying to gain further qualifications. Since their settlement here, less than ten young Hmong have graduated from universities, although most have managed to complete Year 12 in high school and went on to do further vocational training at TAFE colleges. Currently, about half a dozen young men and women are enrolled in bachelor's degree university courses in Cairns, Sydney and Melbourne. It is hoped that this trend will encourage others to follow them.

Conclusion

Where will the Hmong of Australia go to from here? After the first generation, will their children still retain enough of their Hmong cultural heritage to be called Hmong? Or will they be Australian in their hearts and minds, and Hmong only in their appearance? These are questions that many elderly Hmong in Australia, like those in America, are asking themselves. They are wondering whether they have not tried hard enough to change and to fit into their new environment, or whether their children are trying too hard and changing too fast. The big challenges are no longer related to those of economic survival or the accumulation of material assets. Most families are now comfortably off materially, like the majority of the Australian people. What they face and worry more about is the survival of their cultural identity in the midst of the vast ethnic diversity in this country.

The dilemma of how much to retain of their own culture and how much to change to accommodate the demands of the broader community around them is real, and too complex to dwell on here. Many Hmong realise that they need to change, and are already changing in many respects. There can be no turning back to the old times, for even things in the old country they originated from are fast changing. They have enjoyed freedom and many other benefits coming to live in Australia, and are trying to contribute as much as they can to their new country while still following some of their old traditions in order to maintain some kind of cultural identity. The next generation will have to make their own social accommodation and find their own way ahead — probably more as Australians, but perhaps also as Hmong. If the Hmong of north Queensland are any indication of future trends, members of the younger generation will continue to marry within their own community and maintain their mother tongue even while interacting frequently with non-Hmong people and using English most of the time.

Footnotes

[1] With thanks to the Chiang Ching-Kuo Foundation, Taipei, for funding of our recent research in Cairns and Innisfail.

Total Hmong in Australia, 2003

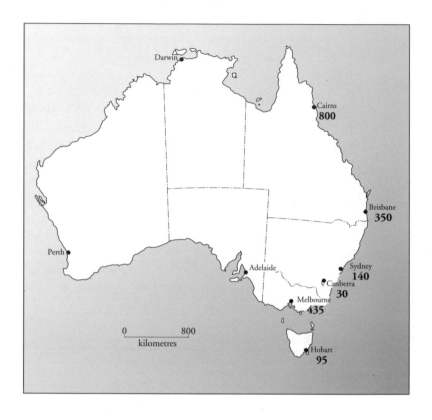

Living Locally, Dreaming Globally

Transnational Cultural Imaginings and Practices in the Hmong Diaspora

Roberta Julian

Introduction

This chapter is part of a larger project exploring the impact of globalisation on Australian national identity. In this chapter I examine identification processes among a small Asian community in Australia by drawing on my research with Hmong in Tasmania. My involvement with the Hmong community in Tasmania began in 1993 when some colleagues and I from the University of Tasmania were approached by Vue Thaow, the first Hmong person to settle in Tasmania, to undertake research on Hmong settlement experiences. We secured funding from the then Bureau of Immigration, Multicultural and Population Research to undertake a study of refugee settlement in Tasmania. This examined the settlement experiences of the largest refugee communities in the state at that time, namely, Hmong, Vietnamese, Chilean, El Salvadoran, Polish and Kurdish (Julian et al. 1997).

Vue Thaow arrived in Tasmania, the small island state at the southeastern tip of Australia, in 1973 as a student under the Colombo Plan. After the fall of Vientiane in 1975, he sponsored his wife and two children to Australia, followed by his parents, his siblings, other members of his clan and then the relatives of those who had married into his clan. Thus began two decades of chain migration of Hmong refugees from Laos to Tasmania, via refugee camps (mainly Ban Vinai) in Thailand. At the turn of the century the emerging Hmong community in Tasmania numbered about 500 and was represented by seven clans. When I met Vue Thaow and the Hmong in Tasmania I began a fascinating journey of discovery of Hmong people who are now dispersed throughout the world; that is, the Hmong diaspora.

This chapter on the Hmong diaspora is based on almost ten years of association with Hmong people — mainly in Tasmania and the United States, but also more recently, in Thailand. I make use of data that has been collected through what could be labelled an ethnographic methodology. This has involved a wide variety of methods: observation, participant observation, in-depth semi-structured interviews, a survey and structured interviews, document analysis (including books, newsletters, articles on the internet, keynote addresses at conferences), analysis of scholarly publications (by Hmong and non-Hmong), autobiographies and biographies of Hmong (such as students and women), cultural artefacts and other media (for example, storycloths or *paj ndau*), plays (for example, 'Highest Mountain Fastest River'), museum displays (for example, 'Hmong of the Mountains'), comedy skits and videos (for example, Tou Ger Xiong's 'Hmong Means Free'), poetry and short stories by Hmong-Americans (for example, in the journal *Paj Ntaub Voice* and the newsletter *Hnub Tshiab*).

The research on which this chapter is based has been guided by two general questions: 'who are the Hmong?' and 'what does it mean to be Hmong?' These questions are of interest to sociologists and anthropologists (for example, Tapp 2000, Schein 1999 and Lee 1996) in that they provide an opportunity to examine processes of identity construction under conditions of postmodernity and in the context of globalisation. Most importantly, however, these questions are of immediate significance to members of the Hmong diaspora themselves. Illustrative of this concern with identity is the fact that the Hmong National Development (HND) conference selected 'The Complexity of Hmong Identity' as its 2002 theme and 'Connecting Across Communities' as its theme for 2004.

Over the past ten years, my interest in the Hmong community has led me to be involved in a wide range of activities relating to Hmong settlement, including presenting papers at the First Hmong National Development Conference in Minneapolis in 1995, the fourth conference held in Denver in 1998 and the seventh held in Milwaukee in 2002. The arguments in this chapter have been rehearsed at these and other sites (such as universities in Thailand) and have benefited from invaluable feedback from Hmong audiences. Nevertheless, the views expressed here remain those of an 'outsider' and are subject to the limitations (as well as the possible strengths) of such a position. I present them here as arguments that are open to debate and contestation and I look forward to a continuing dialogue with Hmong people in various parts of the world on issues relating to Hmong identity.

Globalisation, Diaspora and Identity

This chapter explores the construction of a diasporic Hmong identity in the context of the contradictions of globalism and localism. It argues that the success with which the Hmong are constructing a global identity suggests that the diaspora, as a form of social organisation, has the potential to transcend and succeed the nation-state, thus bridging the gap between the global and the local (compare Cohen 1997). It explores processes of identity construction at four levels: local, national, regional and global. It argues that there are two major foci of identity construction among the Hmong, namely, at the local and the global level, and that rather than being contradictory these processes reinforce one another.

In exploring Hmong identity, it is important to recognise, first, that 'one identity cannot be defined in isolation: the only way to circumscribe an identity is by contrasting it against other

identities. Consequently, *identity* is an ambiguous notion. It gets its
meaning from what it is not, from the Other' (Martin 1995: 6).
Furthermore, it 'requires the presence of the Other, that is, the
perception of someone different and the establishment of a
relationship with him/her/them' (Martin 1995: 6). Thus, as Martin
(1995: 16) argues 'identity, far from being a state characterising
isolated groups, is a *construction in progress* which brings meaning
and value (positive or negative) to a relationship or a set of
relationships with Others' (my emphasis).

Stuart Hall argues that globalisation has 'the effect of
contesting and dislocating the centred and "closed" identities of a
national culture' (1992: 309). He defines globalisation as 'those
processes, operating on a global scale, which cut across national
boundaries, integrating and connecting communities and
organisations in new space-time combinations, making the world
in reality and in experience more interconnected' (1992: 299).
A definition by Rex points even more directly to the possibility of
emergent forms of social organisation resulting from globalisation.
For Rex, globalisation refers to a process in which 'the bounding of
social life by such political units as nation-states has been
superseded by a state of affairs, in which the social relations and
networks in which individuals are involved, as well as the cultural
influences to which they are subject, tend to have global, rather
than purely national character' (Rex 1995: 21–2). For Cohen
diasporas are 'particularly adaptive forms of social organisation'
(1997: 176) in the age of globalisation.

Globalisation and transnational ties open up new sets of
relationships for Hmong people which destabilise the taken-for-
grantedness of past relationships. They thus challenge previous
identities. Globalisation means identity change. As with all
communities, however, it is important to recognise that diasporas
are not unified and homogeneous. As Avtar Brah (1996: 184) has
noted, they are 'lived and re-lived through multiple modalities' as
'differentiated, heterogeneous and contested spaces, even as they
are implicated in the construction of a common "we"'.

So who is engaged in this (re)construction of Hmong
identity in the 'age of globalisation'? Who are the participants? In

what ways does their participation direct the process of identity construction and the content(s) of emergent Hmong identities? The construction of national and cultural identities is often examined only from the point of view of those in power. However, as Denis-Constant Martin has pointed out:

> It takes political brokers *and* ordinary people … to tangle strategies and feelings into a narrative which will raise an echo (1995: 11).

This chapter examines the dynamic interplay between *who* is participating and the emergent *meanings* of Hmong identity that result from their participation. More specifically, it focuses on the role of Hmong women in the (re)construction of Hmong identities in the diaspora.

Hmong Identification Processes

Following Goffman (1959), I wish to focus my discussion on the 'work' being done by Hmong with respect to identity; that is, the presentation of self or more broadly 'identity work'. This concept highlights the fact that identity construction is not just about the development of appropriate narratives, but also (and some would argue, fundamentally) involves social action in the context of established and emergent social relationships. In other words, there is a very important, but often overlooked, performative dimension to identification.

To feed back into the issues raised earlier I will analyse this 'identity work' at four different levels (inter-related empirically): local, national, regional and global. In examining identity construction it is worth acknowledging that '[identity] narratives means being meant for others as well as oneself, several versions of the same narrative may be uttered, or … the same narrative may comprise several levels, because it aims at different targets' (Martin 1995: 8). The analysis here is based on the example of the Tasmanian Hmong. Furthermore:

> … (a)n individual can change his identifications in the course of his life; that is, he may, at a time, feel more

concerned by, more attracted to one particular identity
narrative and, at another time, by another. The same
individual can, at the same time, relate to several
narratives and, to a certain extent, cope with the
contradictions between them. As a matter of fact,
multiple identification is the rule. Identifications are
usually nested like Russian dolls, although the intensity
with which individuals identify to groups and narratives
is variable' (Martin 1995: 14).

The following discussion of identification processes among
the Hmong adopts a framework of multiple identification. Not only
does it recognise the existence of multiple sites of identification (for
example, ethnic, familial, gendered, occupational) but it recognises
the existence of several layers, or levels, of ethnic identification. I will
begin my discussion of Hmong identity at the local level, followed
by the national, regional and global levels. See Table 1 opposite.

'Identity Work': The Local Level

In Tasmania, the work that goes into identity construction at the
local level is predominantly understood in terms of 'maintaining
cultural identity' as encouraged in government policy statements
on Australian multiculturalism (for example, OMA 1989). In the
political context, this is largely carried out by male leaders in the
Hmong community. In this endeavour, they are supported by
migrant support workers. This work predominantly involves
presenting the Hmong community, as Hmong, to Tasmanians and
generating a positive and acceptable image to the Tasmanian
people. Given Tasmania's reliance on tourism, it is perhaps not
surprising that this 'identity work' tends to construct Hmong
identity as 'the exotic Other', as a marketable tourist commodity.

This encourages an essentialist notion of Hmong identity
which homogenises what is, despite its small size, an heterogeneous
'community'. This homogenising process is evident in the words of
a young Hmong man who, when asked what it means to be
Hmong, gave the following response:

Table 1: Hmong Identification Processes

Level	Identity	Processes of Identity Construction
Global	Hmong	• Diasporic identity • Directed by Hmong in the US • Essentialist and based on a 'reinvented' tradition • International marriages • Women as agents of social change • young people and popular culture • eg. identity construction via the internet
Regional	Asian	• Asian identity within Australia • Victims of discrimination vs. the 'Asian' face of Tasmania • Links with Laotians but not with Vietnamese • Regional identity undeveloped • Limited ties with Laos
National	Australian? Hmong-Australian?	• majority (78%) are Australian citizens • Australian identity non-existant • Hmong-Australian identity problematic • limited participation in Australian society • social closure • few Hmong-Australian relationships • second generation assimilating
Local	Hmong	• Maintaining 'cultural identity' • The 'exotic other' • Cultural identity as a marketable commodity • Essentialist • Grounded in a patriarchal clan structure • Endogamous • Women as cultural icons • Hmong identity — commodified, trivialised and marginalised • Resistance from young women

There is definitely less freedom in Hmong culture. It's not like a class system but it is like a caste system. Individuals have their own place and roles to play. The father of the family has the final decision-making. The mother's role is to look after the children and the children's role is to achieve things they are expected to achieve, like school and to respect their elders ... Freedom to us is like freedom but in quotes.

The Hmong identity is remembered and reconstructed in Australia as an essentialist identity. Furthermore, it is grounded in a patriarchal clan structure. Thus to 'maintain cultural identity' implies the maintenance of the Hmong clan structure. The strategies have been very successful thus far. In Australia, there have been almost no out-marriages to date.

It is important to note, however, that the clan takes on a new meaning in the context of constructing a Hmong identity in Australia. As a Hmong man explains:

We live in Australia and I think that clan struggle will not exist any more because we will not have a powerful clan or group who can do politics or that sort of thing. Basically we are looking at clan support. We are looking at the word 'Hmong' as brother to cover everyone. We are looking for people in the Hmong society to raise the status of the whole community.

While some have argued that the significance of the clan is weakening in Australia, I would argue that we are witnessing a transformation in the meaning of the clan in light of attempts to construct an homogeneous Hmong community that 'fits' the exigencies of Australian multiculturalism in practice (compare Hage 1998).

Hmong femininity is constructed to support this clan structure and the image of the 'exotic Other'. Women become the bearers of cultural tradition — cultural icons whose images are a marketable commodity. The symbolic site of this process is Salamanca Market in Hobart, a major tourist attraction. One of the successful economic projects among some Hmong in Hobart

Hmong women selling vegetables at Salamanca market, Hobart, 1997. *Photography by Roberta Julian.*

has been the establishment of small market gardens. The vegetables are sold on Saturdays at the market by groups of Hmong women and children who are popular subjects of the 'tourist gaze' (Urry 2002). Many visitors to Hobart would have a photograph or two of 'the Hmong at Salamanca' in their memoirs.

For Tasmanians, the Hmong at Salamanca Market symbolise a new openness to Asia, a 'new' Tasmanian identity which is inclusive of those of Asian origin. Importantly, the happy faces at the market lead Tasmanians to assume the Hmong have integrated 'easily'. This image belies the economic hardships and settlement difficulties experienced by almost all the Hmong. Nevertheless, it is a successful identity narrative which receives support from Hmong leaders as it indicates acceptance by Tasmanians.

Insofar as the Hmong are accepted as Tasmanians, however, their identity has become commodified, trivialised and marginalised. It is a superficial Hmong identity that is understood and accepted as part of the Tasmanian cultural landscape. Thus many Hmong continue to feel that they are misunderstood in their attempts to deal with mainstream service providers. They therefore continue to seek opportunities to engage in a 'presentation of self' on their own terms. This leads into a national strategy which I will address below.

In short, at the local level 'identity work' focuses on 'maintaining cultural identity'; that is, on maintaining an 'authentic' Hmong identity in an Australian context. This identity is essentialist. It is largely controlled by male leaders and is subsequently resisted and renegotiated by Hmong youth, particularly young women. Tasmanians have accepted a superficial, trivialised version of Hmong identity to incorporate into their newly emerging 'identity with many faces', one of which is an Asian face (considered essential for the tourist market).

The Hmong community's struggle to establish liminal sites for a more 'authentic' local Hmong identity reflects the process of identity construction at various levels. Suggested sites include the development of a 'traditional' Hmong village as a tourist attraction, and the establishment of a Hmong burial site in a valley about forty minutes out of Hobart.

'Identity Work': The National Level

In the late 1990s, 78 per cent of the Hmong in Hobart were either Australian citizens or had applied for Australian citizenship (Julian et al. 1997: 48). To what extent do they identify as Australian? What does it mean to be Australian for the Hmong in Hobart?

The short answer is that the Hmong in Hobart, at least, do not identify as Australian. Unlike in other areas of Hmong settlement in Australia, they have minimal interaction with other Australians. Most adults do not work and most children mix with other Hmong at school. For example, when discussing his friends outside the Hmong community a young man noted:

> But those friends are not personal friends. We might have something in common but I still feel detached when I am with them. The things that they do still do not feel right with me.

The Hobart Hmong constitute a close-knit community which is isolated from the wider society. As one Hmong man stated:

> He says [as] for Australian friends, he doesn't speak much English and [so] doesn't have many. But with the Hmong, everyone is good to everyone. (Through interpreter.)

As a result of limited English language skills they have limited access to information. In the words of a Hmong man:

> In Laos I like to listen to the radio and read the newspaper to understand and know what was happening ... but when we came to Australia we watch the TV but we don't understand and don't know anything that is going on ...

When they must deal with Australian institutions many find these bewildering and some have difficulty understanding Australia's social and political system. As a consequence, many do not feel a sense of security about the future. Rather, they express fear and uncertainty with respect to future government changes evident in, for example, recent concerns over the suggestion that welfare payments may disappear in the future. In short, they fit well Schutz's (1974) description of 'the stranger'.

The lack of autonomy and control experienced by Hmong men in Hobart expresses itself most dramatically in a pervasive anxiety about the future. This is evident first in a strong concern over whether their own security as welfare recipients can be maintained indefinitely in the context of changing governments, and secondly in their recognition that their children are changing to fit into a society and a future that they cannot envision. The following quotations are indicative of these views:

> He said he came here to settle but because he doesn't speak the language it is hard. And he doesn't know what to do. He lives like this every day. He doesn't know about the future or what will happen. He feels worried. (Through interpreter.)

> The children act differently here than how they grow up in Laos … They go to school, they learn different things than they learn in Laos. In Laos they grow up and they stay home with you … Also in Laos they can help the parents.

> Two main problems. Firstly, the language. If you don't speak so well you need someone to go with you. And secondly, you rely on social security money. If they stop one day and don't pay, how are you going to survive?

> Our biggest worry is the children … whether they will be able to learn at school, and whether after school they will be able to get a job … And also our biggest problem is because we don't know the language we don't know how we're going to be in a few years time.

On the other hand, those who arrived as young men and women and were educated in Tasmania demonstrate a greater degree of confidence with respect to planning for the future. As one man stated:

> Lots of plans for the future. I want the Australian government to recognise that we were part of the contingency for the Vietnam War and I want our people

to march on Anzac Day as part of that group. I want us to be able to practise our rituals openly and share it with everyone rather than behind closed doors ... I also want all my people to be self-sufficient and independent of social welfare.

Despite such expressed ideals, the construction of a hybrid Hmong-Australian identity is problematic. Pride in Hmong culture is commonly expressed. However, in the current situation, it is felt difficult, if not impossible, to be Hmong and Australian simultaneously because some Hmong practices are illegal. Importantly, many of these 'illegal' practices are those considered central to Hmong identity. The illegal status of these practices thus constitutes a major barrier to what is seen as 'becoming Australian'. The difficulties experienced in this endeavour are illustrated in the following comments:

Some [customs] we haven't been able to continue because of Australian laws but some we can do ... There is a problem that we sometimes need to use live animals for some of our practices. The animals are used to find lost spirits. It is not sacrifice.

We are trying to submit some documents to the government for this kind of approval. It is still very difficult for us because the [Hmong] community in Australia is still very small. The practices here are not well known. In America there are more people who have cured a number of American people and my feeling is that if we could access those people it would be very helpful.

At the core of Hmong culture lies a system of religious beliefs and practices that is intertwined with holistic medicine. In explaining this belief system, a Hmong person used the analogy of a car and its driver. He explained that if sickness occurs, it could mean:

... one of our spirits has got lost or that one of our spirits has been injured ... We try to heal the spirit first ... Let me use the analogy of a car ... The driver is like the spirit.

If the driver got lost the car can't move anymore. So
somebody must find the driver of the car so it can move
again.

Thus, to a large extent, the maintenance of Hmong culture
is dependent upon the maintenance of Hmong health and
religious practices. The Hmong recognise that, in a multicultural
society, such practices need to be integrated into the Australian
way of life. They are therefore keen for Anglo-Australians to
embrace their holistic health practices, if not the religious beliefs
that underlie them. This is clearly evident in the following
quotations from interviews with Hmong in Hobart:

> Probably the most important thing to me is to be allowed
> to practise our religion freely without any restrictions …
> That is what I want and that is what I think every Hmong
> member here wants.

> My biggest thing in life is to be able to say: 'This is my
> culture, this is why we practise it and this is the reason we
> believe it. You are welcome to come and join it if you
> believe in shamanism. If you are sick our shaman is there
> to perform it if you want it.' That is the kind of message.

> To be honest with you there are some practices that we are
> unable to do … For example, if somebody dies we have to
> leave the body exposed for one or two days and we can't
> do that. So we have to change that. The grave has to be in
> a certain position with a certain mountain so that when
> the person is reincarnated into his or her future they have
> a much more beneficial life. We have to change that too
> … The way you face a dead person is important. There
> has to be a mountain at the end to rest his foot on and a
> mountain at the back to rest his head on and a mountain
> on the side so he can reach for it. This is very important
> for a Hmong person.

At the national level, the Hmong have explored strategies
aimed at exposing Anglo-Australians to the benefits of their
healing practices. They have thus embarked on a project which

involves defining their practices in such a way that they are encompassed under the rubric of 'alternative medicine'. This is perceived as one way of legitimising the practices central to the Hmong which, if accepted more widely, may create a space for the emergence of a Hmong-Australian identity.

'Identity Work': The Regional Level

Historically, the Australian identity has been constructed with Asians as the 'Other' (Ip et al. 1994, Ang 2000). The White Australia policy was not officially abandoned until the mid 1970s. With increased Asian immigration to Australia since the 1970s, the 'Other' is now clearly visible within our national boundaries, as recent political events within Australia have made clear. This raises significant challenges for the reconstruction of an Australian national identity that acknowledges Australia's geographical location in the Asia–Pacific region.

The Hmong in Australia are aware that they are viewed as Asian. In addition, they are aware that 'Asians' are often viewed negatively, whereas the Hmong are viewed positively. Day-to-day interaction with Asians is often discriminatory and racist. This is partly why, at a local level, the Hmong are at pains to establish a clearly defined *Hmong* identity.

However, the Hmong leaders are also politically astute. Politics is also part of being Hmong. They were politically active in Laos and they continue to be politically active in 'the West'. They are aware of their status as a very small ethnic minority with low socio-economic status. They are struggling to improve their status as a community. In doing so, they are aware that they need to grow. This has been part of the motivation for continued sponsorship of Hmong from Thai refugee camps (until the final closure of the camps in 1995).

In addition, they have invited Laotian immigrants to Hmong functions. In Melbourne, some Hmong have married some Laotians. However, many Hmong state that they wish to distinguish themselves from Vietnamese, almost certainly for political reasons dating back to the conflicts in Laos. Some Hmong

in Hobart have stated that they would prefer not to live in
Melbourne because 'there are too many Vietnamese there'. Links
with Laos have been limited to date because of the unsettled nature
of the political situation. Nevertheless, as the situation calms down
these ties are likely to increase. One family in Tasmania has
recently returned to Laos for a visit.

In short, given the small size of the Hmong communities in
Australia, an Asian identity is being embraced for political
purposes, although historical antipathies remain which make the
construction of an inclusive Asian identity problematic. The Asian
identity constructed by the Hmong is a contingent one.

'Identity work': The Global Level

Since 1975 Hmong refugees have settled in the United States,
France, Australia, Canada and French Guiana. There are also
Hmong in China, Thailand and Vietnam.

When I originally began exploring the question 'who are
the Hmong?' I discovered a highly visible, well articulated and
almost *unitary* narrative. The same story emerged in books and
videos, as well as in interviews with Hmong in Australia and in the
United States. I would argues that this is a hegemonic discourse
emanating from Hmong-America which is adopted by Hmong
throughout the diaspora. Hmong leaders in the United States
organise national and international conferences on an annual basis
and have earned the support of politicians and academics. They
communicate with Hmong throughout the world and are eager to
construct a unified Hmong identity at this level.

Gary Yia Lee, an Australian Hmong with a PhD in
anthropology, articulates this goal clearly in one of his articles on
the internet:

> The ability to travel freely to other countries where
> Hmong live and the informal Hmong mass media have
> allowed the Hmong people to rediscover each other, to
> see each other on videos.

The Hmong, no matter where they are, need to know that the total sum is always bigger than its parts: the overall global Hmong identity is greater than its many local differences and groups ... The biggest challenge for all Hmong is ... to turn our diverse language and customs into one unified and one Hmong/Miao identity ... (Lee 1996).

So, what precisely are the characteristics of this global identity narrative? Who is involved in its construction?

The dominant identity narrative could be described as the quintessential 'refugee story' — a version of the well known 'immigrant success story'. It is a 'heroic' narrative that incorporates a number of themes:

- the war and the military (the starting point for the diasporic narrative);

- the refugee experience (including flight across the Mekong River and languishing in Thai refugee camps for many years);

- continuity with the past through recognition of the value of clan ties and 'traditional' Hmong culture (for example, shamanism);

- symbols of movement into the future (the modern or the postmodern) by emphasising the many educational achievements there have been.

The War and the Military

In this dominant narrative, Hmong identity is forged on a past relationship with the United States in Laos. The Hmong are provided with a unique identity *vis-à-vis* America, establishing and reinforcing a relationship of patronage. In general, this has been a successful strategy for Hmong-Americans, 'voiced' loudest and most articulately by Hmong male elites. It is often articulated in books about the Hmong in America, as illustrated in the following opening paragraph, based on the translation of an interview with a Hmong man, Chia Koua Xiong:

Who are the Hmong?

In Laos, we helped you fight the war. The Americans came to live with our leaders in our country ... We provided food ... If the Americans came to our house, whatever we ate we treated the Americans equally ... If we found an injured soldier ... we ... carried the American to the base ... In some dangerous situations we were willing to let ten Hmong soldiers die so that one of your leaders could live ...

We considered Americans as our own brothers ... Now we have lost our own country ... Those who made it here, they have the opportunity for education and jobs ... We started a new life so that our children would have a better life (Pfaff 1995: 7).

Numerous videos and books recount the same story of the Hmong exodus from Laos to resettlement in the West: first, of a 'brotherhood' with United States' citizens as a consequence of fighting side by side in the Vietnam War; and second, of 'successful' adaptation to American society (evidenced by educational success) alongside the maintenance of 'traditional' cultural practices (such as shamanism).

There are two popular heroes of this narrative, in particular, who are often taken to represent the link with the past and the move into the future, although of course there are other elite Hmong leaders in Thailand, Vietnam and China. Both of these now reside in the United States. The first is General Vang Pao, acknowledged leader of the Hmong diaspora, who symbolises the military basis of the Hmong identity. The other hero is Dr Yang Dao, the first Hmong to receive a doctorate of philosophy, who is considered the patron of Hmong education and symbolises the way ahead.

While this narrative is predominantly articulated by male elites, it is also enacted and perpetuated by ordinary men and women. For example, women have reproduced this narrative in the 'storycloth' (*paj ndau*), a form of needlework first made around 1976 in Ban Vinai refugee camp (Anderson 1996: 30). Commonly, the storycloths chronicle village life in the mountains of Laos, depict religious ceremonies, or illustrate Hmong folktales. The majority created in the 'West' or for the Western market, however, recount the transition from village life prior to the war, through the escape from Laos after the war, to life in refugee camps in Thailand and often 'end' with an image of the plane in Bangkok that was to take them to 'freedom' in the United States. As Anderson (1996: 28) states:

> The storycloths are a link with the past. They are shared memories captured in visual images, with the embroiderer's needle rather than the camera or the written word. As episodes of social history, they record and pass on information about Hmong customs to the younger generation, especially those born in the United States with no first-hand knowledge of Laos ... They are a form of non-verbal communication that transcend [sic] language barriers (1996: 28).

The Refugee Experience

Public events involving Hmong almost always contain accounts of refugees enduring forced migration. Typical is the following keynote speech, from the Fourth Annual National Hmong Conference held in Denver, Colorado in April 1998. Dr Mymee Her, a young Hmong psychologist from California, declared:

> The Hmong are classified as REFUGEES ... Hmong refugees come to the United States wounded. Most have been beaten up physically and emotionally. They seek out shelter from whatever country will offer them safety. They have no anticipation of what life holds for them in the country of refuge. They are in a state of shock, not realising what had just happened (Her 1998).

The main focus of such narratives is on maintaining continuity with the past while taking advantage of opportunities for educational and material success in the West. Thus, Her began her speech by intoning:

When I was asked to deliver a keynote address ... I was
told that the conference theme was living the American
dream. I was ecstatic, relieved that for once I did not have
to talk about the struggles and suffering of the Hmong
people ... But as I sat down to think about what I was
going to say ... [I realised that it is] impossible to talk
about our people living the American dream without
talking about the history that has brought us to America,
including the struggles and sufferings everyone must
endure as part of our American Dream ...

From these experiences she identifies the key characteristics
of Hmong identity as those of resilience, family, adaptability, and
humility. She remembers her father's description of bamboo in the
wind, quoting his words:

A bamboo is a very thin tree, but it is a very strong tree. It
has deep roots so that it will not be uprooted by strong
wind, and its stem is flexible enough to bend in the wind.

She draws on this metaphor to describe the central
characteristics of Hmong identity in the United States:

My father urged me to be like the bamboo in my
approach to life. Firmly planted in my own opinions and
truths, yet flexible enough to hear what others, including
my mother, have to say without breaking or feeling I had
everything to lose. I think this is the mind set of the
Hmong people, flexible enough to adapt to change, yet
firmly planted by its roots to never tip over or break ...

Family, adaptability, and humility. These are the
characteristics that I think are the threads which have held
us together as a nation of Hmong. And these are the
threads which I think will help us endure as a people,
living the American Dream.

In this narrative, the refugee experience has become central
to the meaning of Hmongness in the West. The significance of this
is illustrated in Her's own life history. Having married an Iranian-
American, she is often asked how she deals with their differences

(such as religious differences). She states that she sees their shared refugee status as a unifying experience and that she has come to see this refugee experience as a defining feature of Hmong identity. On this basis she describes her husband as 'a Hmong man in the skin of an Iranian'.

Continuity with the Past While Embracing the Future: Reinventing 'Tradition'

On the one hand, the narratives recounted here support and reinforce an essentialist notion of Hmongness and encourage the maintenance of ideas of 'tradition' and 'authenticity'. On the other hand, they acknowledge the impact of 'new' experiences (such as forced migration) on the Hmong identity as a *construction in progress*.

This contestation over 'tradition' and its value in the context of the diaspora is evident in debates about the importance of the clan to Hmong culture.[1] The is clearly apparent in the following comments from a Hmong leader in Australia:

> I think clan structure and clan influence is still very strong. We keep trying to say that it should not be regarded as that strong. But it will be very hard to break that. Firstly people are so used to it. Secondly because of the clan structure the clan is interdependent. If you are my clan and I come to you with a problem you can't really refuse it. On that basis the relationship has not died. The reason we are not progressing so quickly is because we regard the clan structure as so important ... People will serve their clan first. If I was looking for someone I would look around my clan first, then go to the next closest clan. If we look at it as a practical issue it is bad. If we look at it as a social issue I don't think there is anything in the world better than the Hmong social structure ...
>
> We say, please don't regard the clan structure as so important. That is why we are so backward ...
>
> This clan will not die. We say it is not important but it is truly important in our hearts.

Men's strategies in relation to marriage further reinforce 'traditional' social ties in the diaspora. A number of young Hmong men in the United States have asked me: 'How traditional are young Hmong women in Australia?' For many of these young men, their inquiries preface comments about their desire to marry more 'traditional' Hmong women than the educated, assertive, and self-assured Hmong women they meet in the United States. Rising educational levels bring these issues to the fore.

When 'traditional' Hmongness is emphasised, those in the West attempting to reconstruct it look to Thailand and Laos for 'authenticity'. For many young Hmong, visits to northern Thailand and Laos are viewed with enthusiasm and are encouraged by parents as a way of reclaiming traditional Hmongness. For some Hmong men in the West, marrying Thai Hmong women is a way of maintaining traditional Hmongness. It can be argued that the maintenance of such connections with the past involves a *reinvention* of tradition which takes the form of a 'strategic essentialism' (Spivak 1990, Ang 1993).

Paradoxically, this strategy serves to both inhibit and encourage change in cultural practices. For example, 'traditional' views of Hmong femininity are sustained, as Hmong women are expected to be the bearers of cultural tradition (see Julian 1998, Ganguly-Scrase and Julian 1999). So, too, gender inequalities that existed in Laos remain unchallenged. On the other hand, emphasis on links with the past has led to the (re)discovery of Hmong 'roots' in China (Schein 2000) and a consequent process of sinicisation of contemporary Hmong identity (Tapp 2000). One of the dominant signifiers of this sinicised Hmong identity is the Chinese Hmong costume, which has been increasingly adopted by young Hmong women at New Year celebrations throughout the diaspora. Significantly, the Chinese Hmong skirt is now mass-produced in China and exported to Hmong women worldwide who wear it in favour of the hand-made skirts that their mothers laboured over (Wronska-Friend, this volume). There is, in this global flow, a universalisation of a different kind of Hmong identity.

While it has greatest strategic value in the local contexts of various states in the United States, this diasporic identity is also evident among Hmong on the diaspora's periphery, particularly in

Canada, France and Australia. The boundaries of this 'imagined community' (Anderson 1983), though, are not spatial; they are grounded in the social networks that constitute the diaspora. This is evidenced by the fact that this global narrative resonates with some Hmong in Bangkok (who communicate regularly on the internet with Hmong in the United States) and in Wat Tam Krabok (where Hmong are in receipt of financial remittances from Hmong in the United States) but not with Hmong hill-tribes in northern Thailand (Ralana Maneeprasert, personal communication, 2001).

Counter-Hegemonic Discourses

The previous section has demonstrated the existence of a unitary 'global' Hmong identity emanating from Hmong-America, one that is in evidence throughout the Hmong diaspora. However, at the global level it is also possible to identify resistances and/or challenges to the hegemonic discourse, and it cannot be said that the voices of American Hmong represent all those overseas. Such resistances arise where the narrative of the 'refugee success story' does not resonate with lived experience. The voices that arise in local contexts (both inside and outside the United States) reflect differences within the Hmong diaspora based on gender, age, class, religion, 'migrantness' and place. They are what Werbner (1998: 12) refers to as voices of 'argument and imaginative creativity'.

The voices of resistance are predominantly those of educated Hmong women. However, they have been joined more recently by the voices of Hmong youth, both male and female. The main topics of contestation and debate include clan structure, youthful marriage, cross-cultural marriage, polygamy and levirate, 'kidnap' marriages, women's education, and the significance of Hmong language for Hmong identity. New communications media, such as the internet, provide a means of reaching a global Hmong audience. There is an online Hmong journal and at least one Hmong home page in both America and Australia. Young Hmong people in the United States, Australia, Canada, Thailand and Laos discuss issues surrounding Hmong identity in various chat rooms.

The field of popular culture is a newly emerging and extremely significant site for the expression of these voices.

Consider Tou Ger Xiong, a freelance dramatic artist and stand-up comedian. His use of rap to narrate and 'translate' Hmongness not only creates an identification with African-Americans, but posits Hmong as racial minority, rather than refugee (compare Hein 1994). Tou Ger Xiong's message of Hmongness sounds like this:

> As you can see I'm Asian; yeah, I'm not black.
> What I'm about to say might sound like slack,
> But just lend me your ears, and hear me out,
> I've come to tell you what I'm all about.
> Yes my name is Tou, and I've come to say
> That I'm special, talented in many ways.
> Yes I know kung fu, and martial arts,
> You try to go get me, man I'll tear you apart.
> Yeah I'm bad, mean, and tough is my game.
> They call me the master; yes, it's my name.
>
> Well you might think it's weird, to see that I'm Asian,
> Busking some rhymes on such an occasion.
> Well let me tell you, how I came to be,
> I was born in Laos in seventy-three.
> In my culture, we sing and dance,
> But I'm a style rapper, yeah I take my chance.
> Yo, even though this, is my first rap,
> You don't have to like it, and you don't have to clap.
> To those who listen, it might be nice,
> To see this Hmong boy, kickin' like Vanilla Ice
> (Xiong 1998).

This perception of racial minority resonates strongly with many young Hmong in the United States. No longer defining themselves as refugees, their performances at the 2002 Hmong National Development Conference Youth Forum in Milwaukee placed a wide range of popular cultural acts on display — from break dancing to poetry.

Hmong Women and the (re)Construction of Hmong Identity

Hmong women play a leading role in the process of 'translating' Hmongness as they resist, challenge and negotiate new constructions of Hmong femininity. For example, in 1996, a small group of young Hmong women in the United States organised themselves and then raised enough funds to enable them to attend the non-government organisations' Women's Conference in Beijing (as representatives of Hmong women throughout the world). Vang (1994: 35) discusses in some depth the ways in which Hmong in the United States have responded to young married Hmong women who have bachelor degrees and also play important roles in both Hmong and American communities. As she argues, these new female roles challenge traditional notions of femininity and masculinity thereby threatening traditional male dominance.

The processes of negotiating and constructing new identities among Hmong women occur in a wide range of social contexts. Notions of 'culture' and 'tradition' are contested not only within the private sphere but within the domains of public life: in schools, at work, in the politics of multiculturalism. More importantly, I would argue that women, rather than only being the bearers of some fixed and static 'traditional' culture, are also crucial agents in the process of reconstructing new meanings of Hmonghood. Their daily involvement in a wide range of institutional contexts leads some Hmong women to constantly challenge the gendered power relations at the core of Hmong social organisation (Donnelly 1994). Such challenges occur at all levels of social life: the interpersonal, the familial, the communal, the wider society and the global. Significantly, negotiations over the meaning of 'Hmongness' are taking place in all the countries in the West in which Hmong have settled. The transnational character of the diasporic community can thus be viewed as a resource. For example, email communication provides a transnational mechanism for constructions of 'new' Hmong femininity in the diaspora, linking solitary 'trailblazers' (Bays 1994) in Australia with their more numerous counterparts in the United States.

New 'alternative' journals also provide a site for the
construction of alternative or refashioned versions of Hmong
femininity. One of these, *Paj Ntaub Voice*, is subtitled *A Journal
Giving Expression to Hmoob Voices.*[2] In the Winter 2001 edition
entitled 'Silence' the editor, Mai Neng Moua (a writer herself), states:

> When I think of silence, I hear my mother telling me not
> to ask so many questions, to not speak with so much
> passion with my hands and face or in the presence of
> older Hmoob men. I usually associate silence with
> powerlessness, punishment, and control … silence is also
> peace and quiet …
>
> The focus of this issue is silence. The point was to give
> voice to those who had not been heard before, to shed
> light on and talk about issues that have been pushed aside
> or hidden. This task … was in line with *Paj Ntaub Voice*'s
> goals of encouraging Hmoob writers to write their own
> stories and create their own images of themselves …
>
> Writing and publishing for Hmoob writers are courageous
> acts … Moving from saying nothing to expression, to
> shouting and loudness takes courage. It is, to borrow bell
> hook's expression, an 'act of resistance' — of refusing to
> remain silent, or rejecting the stories and images others
> have created of us, of refusing to lie down and die quietly,
> of 'talking back' (2001: 4).

Paj Ntaub Voice thus creates a space for the reconstruction
of Hmong identity; it can serve as a tool for offering resistance and
challenging the meaning of 'tradition'. This is evident in the
following excerpt from *Paj Ntaub Voice*:

> It is disturbingly ironic that although Hmong means
> 'free', the majority of us feel just the opposite, 'trapped'.
> How then, can we be Hmong? The truth is, how we lived
> in China, Laos, and Thailand cannot explain what we feel
> or justify who we are today in America. This discrepancy
> clearly confirms that we must redefine Hmong in the
> context of our contemporary issues (Cha 2001: 8).

The following poem published in the same journal expresses another young Hmong woman's oppositional positioning in relation to her Hmong identity.

Everyday.
Between personal and professional:
The world does not consist
Of Hmong issues alone.
Even though they hit closer to home.
There is no global, 'bigger' picture
In the Hmong community.
We're all struggling.

It hurts to read the paper these days.
Between individual, family and community
Because I am a lone Hmong woman
I'm appreciated more outside of the home.
My individuality is validated.
I'm expected to compete.

Not for affection.

While my sister waits to have
A late night conversation with me,
And the dishes lie dirty in the sink.
Letters unanswered.
One more meal with the relatives, missed.

One less argument I get to hear.

Between sinner and saint:
The amorphous, ever-present double standard
That slips unacknowledged to the back of our minds.
The 'good Hmong girl' façade
I will never be able to live up to
Believe me, I've tried.
For 18 years, I've tried.
And the label I now carry
In private, in jest …
Just another day (Yang 2001: 46).

The importance of such sites is also evident in the opening paragraph of a contribution to *Hnub Tshiab*, a Hmong women's publication:

> As I thought of this article, many of the issues I have faced as a single Hmong woman in her mid-twenties came to mind. Should I discuss the functional reasons why marriage is so important in the Hmong culture, especially for women? Or do I talk about the lack of eligible, older Hmong men? Better yet, should I complain about the attempts by my relatives to find me a good husband as if it were an unfortunate circumstance that I was single instead of a conscious choice? Thinking it over, though, I decided that all those questions boiled down to one fundamental truth — the Hmong community is still trying to learn how to treat the increasing number of Hmong women who, like me, are making the choice to stay single in their mid-twenties (Yang 2002: 1).

The voices of Hmong women and young people are also being heard in other arenas such as theatres and art galleries. In Minneapolis, Minnesota, the new 'Theater Mu' has become an avenue for Hmong actors and Hmong plays, and in April 2002, an alternative art gallery held an exhibition of works by Hmong-American artists.

Importantly, an examination of the process of identity construction among Hmong women demonstrates the collective nature of these resistant and oppositional positionings (see Hall 1976/2002). Gigi Durham (1999) has criticised the common formulations of resistance among young women that often, and inappropriately, adopt a model of autonomous individuals constructing resistant readings of dominant discourses. On the contrary, she argues that this overlooks 'the crucial role of women's relationships with other women in their constructions of social reality' (1999: 215). Many of the strategies discussed above demonstrate the successful translation of Hmong identity through the collective activities of Hmong youth, especially young women.

The success of these strategies is evident in their impact on cultural practices. This is exemplified by 'The Sounders', a musical group whose first album, *Leej Twg Lub Paj Rose*, was released in 1994. In the first edition of the *Hmong American Journal*, journalist Pa Houa Lee explained:

> They are considered by many as one of the pioneers of modern Hmong music due to the music they have created. Before Sounders, most Hmong parties were conducted in a structured and orderly manner. Eligible young women would sit in chairs at the front of the audience. When each song begins [sic], the men would go up and find an available partner to dance with ...

> Then came Sounders. With their non-traditional music, they have forever changed the way Hmong parties are conducted. Their music demands new moves. Their music demands new ways of getting into and out of the dance floors quickly. For the first year or so, people were confused and wondered if they should adapt to this new music or if they should just ignore parties totally.

> But then, Sounder's music became more and more enticing and before they knew it, all the front chairs disappeared and the ladies were no longer 'just available' for the convenience of men ...

> As time went on and people started catching up to Sounder's innovative music, new rules were made. Now everyone is just there [at the concert] to dance and party the night away ... (2002: 36).

This brief analysis has provided evidence of dissonant, resistant, vibrant Hmong 'voices' that may run counter to the hegemonic discourse identified earlier. Unlike the hegemonic discourse that attempts to impose a unitary Hmong identity throughout the diaspora, counter-hegemonic discourses are marked by fragmentation and multiplicity.

As Hmong women respond to the economic and social processes of resettlement and challenge 'traditional' notions of Hmong womanhood they are clearly participating as active agents in the construction of an emergent Hmong identity in the diaspora. This global identity transcends local and national identities. It emerges out of a global, 'transcendent' lived experience while, at the same time, it is implicated in the very performance of Hmong identities at the local level.

Conclusions

Hmong Identification in Australia

In the introduction, I quoted from Denis-Constant Martin who stated: 'It takes political brokers *and* ordinary people ... to tangle strategies and feelings into a narrative which will raise an echo' (1995: 11) and I raised the question: who is participating in the construction of contemporary Australian identity?

I would argue that ethnic minorities need to be engaged in the process of identity construction at a national level if a new, inclusive Australian identity is to be constructed. My analysis of identity construction among the Hmong suggests that at this point, it can be argued that at least some, if not the majority, are not. The politics of Australian identity is predominantly in the hands of Anglo-Australian power brokers.

As we have seen, for the Hmong (as for many other ethnic minorities in Australia) there are a number of factors (associated with their class position) which exclude them from participating in the construction of a 'new' inclusive Australian identity. These include high rates of unemployment, limited English language ability, no access to information, and limited opportunities for interaction with Anglo-Australians, all of which contribute to the selection of adaptive strategies which serve to reinvent Hmong (ethnic) tradition in such a way that it increases the level of social closure characteristic of the ethnic community.

Limited participation in Australian society means that rather than contributing to a change in the meaning of Australian identity, the majority are not in a position to forge relationships with Anglo-Australians which create new meanings. Rather, their marginal positions and relative isolation, by leaving the process of identity construction to Anglo-Australians, serve to further reinforce the raced and gendered Australian identity of the past. This suggests that Asian immigration, rather than providing the opportunity for new relationships and identities to emerge, has thus far provided opportunities for the reinforcement /strengthening of Asians as 'Other'.

Identities are not only narratives but are grounded in social relationships. Changing identities are dependent upon changing relationships. Clearly, the construction of a new inclusive Australian identity can only be achieved by addressing issues of *social participation* alongside those of identity construction.

The Hmong Diaspora

The Hmong not only provide a case study of the difficulties associated with taking on an Australian identity as an ethnic minority in Australia; they also suggest a new way of being in advanced modernity/postmodernity. Do they provide the prototype of new identities in which the local and the global claim priority over the national? Do their difficulties in constructing a Hmong-Australian identity suggest that such multiple identities in a multicultural society are not practical? Or do they indicate that multiple identities will shift so easily that they deny labelling?

My analysis of identification processes among the Hmong in Tasmania provides the basis for some tentative but, I believe, interesting observations at the global level. Could it be that the experiences of the Hmong, rather than being indicative of a 'traditional' culture or ethnic community attempting to integrate into the Australian nation, indicate the trends in identity formation in the 'age of globalisation'? (Cohen 1996: 517). Cohen has pointed to the central features of these trends when he writes:

> Certain writers have suggested that a perverse feature of globalization at the cultural level is that it has brought about both the universalization and the fragmentation and multiplication of identities. An identification with a diaspora serves to bridge the gap between the local and the global, even if the outcome is a cultural artefact rather than a political project (Cohen 1996: 516).

Importantly, Hall argues that globalisation has two possible
and alternative effects on cultural identities:

> Some identities gravitate to what Robbins calls 'Tradition',
> attempting to restore their former purity and recover the
> unities and certainties which are felt as being lost. Others
> accept that identity is subject to the play of history,
> politics, representation and difference, so that they are
> unlikely ever again to be 'pure'; and these consequently
> gravitate towards what Robbins (following Homi
> Bhabha) calls 'Translation' (1992: 309).

Significantly, the paradox of the Hmong is that they are
engaged in both processes. It is through a reassertion of 'tradition'
at the global level, together with the resistance and negotiation
undertaken by the next generation (especially women), that new
local Hmong identities are emerging in the context of the diaspora.
Perhaps this is true of all diasporas and contributes to their success
as a form of organisation in the 'age of globalisation'. In the
meantime, for the Hmong, participation in the construction of an
emergent Australian identity, capable of including its traditional
'Other', remains problematic.

To conclude, this chapter has shown the complexity of
Hmong identification processes at local, national, regional and
global levels. It is worth noting at this point, that over the past five
years many of the Hmong have been leaving Tasmania, with the
majority resettling in Queensland. The major reasons for this relate
to greater employment opportunities together with factors relating
to clan politics. These secondary migrations within Australia will
have significant consequences for the contours of the local/global
dimensions of Hmong identity in the diaspora. In the context of
the analysis presented here, such changes highlight the fact that:

Cultural boundaries are not etched in stone but have slippery divisions dependent on the self-adopted labels of groups. What seems clear is that, far from an end to history, or the loss of the subject, identity politics and cultural preservation are going to be among the hottest issues of the next century that will be fought out internationally and intra-nationally, with profound political and economic consequences (Sreberny-Mahommadi 1991: 135).

Footnotes

[1] For example, there are many Hmong who are Christians.

[2] This journal, like the *American Hmong Journal*, is a bilingual production aimed largely at young, educated Hmong. *Noog Liaj Noov Luv*, printed in French Guyana and with contributions from Hmong in France, Laos, Thailand and China, is a truly global Hmong publication (Eds).

Hmong Diaspora in Australia

Nicholas Tapp

Introduction

A Brief Sketch of the Ethnic History of North Queensland

North Queensland has been no stranger to ethnic variety and conflict. After the visits of early explorers, Leichhardt's expedition of 1844–45 had led to a much greater knowledge of the north. Almost every expedition to the region seems to have involved fatal skirmishes with aboriginal inhabitants. Overland squatters started to arrive from the 1850s in search of pasturelands for sheep and cattle, and in 1859 Queensland was formally separated as a colony from New South Wales. Bolton (1963: 53) says that although aboriginal resistance had been successfully quelled within a few years of the coming of the white man, in 1861, incidents continued to occur. In 1889, Carl Lumholtz described how although 'the rough settler, who never sees a woman of his own race, soon begins to associate with the black women', real friendship is impossible: 'the white men shoot the black men, and the black men kill the white men when they can, and spear their sheep and cattle' (1889: 371). Dixon (1983: 53) describes the

horrific nature of the 1897 Queensland Aborigine Protection and
Restriction of the Sale of Opium Act, which authorised their
removal into reserves, forbade them to buy liquor, marry or
cohabit with whites without the permission of the Chief Protector.

Bonded Pacific Island labour was first used on the sheep
farms and on the cotton and sugar plantations from the 1860s,
although the traffic in 'Islanders' was widely condemned by
missionaries. The first gold rush began in 1867 at Cape York, and
increasingly over the next two decades prospectors for valuable
minerals joined the early pastoralists. For some years settlers would
divide their time between mining districts and canefields, but
gradually a large number of ex-miners settled in the sugar districts
(Bolton 1963: 303). A thousand Chinese overlanded from the
south in 1867–68 after news of the gold find at Cape River, and
then from 1875 immigrants from southern China started to arrive
after Queensland gold reached the markets of Canton and Hong
Kong (Bolton 1963: 55). Many of these Chinese migrants stayed
on as cultivators, or as investors in cotton and sugar mills. Market
gardening, of cabbages and lettuce, became a Chinese monopoly in
the 1880s and 1890s (Bolton 1963: 222). They pioneered fruit on
the humid coastal land between Cairns and Innisfail and maize in
the more temperate Atherton Highlands (Bolton 1963: 229). By
1890, the Italians had started to replace Chinese as timber-fellers
on the canefields and as charcoal burners (Bolton 1963: 160). By
1916 Italians outnumbered the Anglo-Irish by about three to one
among the canecutters, from whom new sugar farmers were often
drawn (Bolton 1963: 310). Dixon (1983: 106) describes one small
Italian town (Dimbulah) whose main crop was tobacco, 'with a
few fields of marijuana hidden away …' . Japanese workers were
also important among the canecutters, arriving in Geraldton
(Innisfail after 1910) in 1889 after the suspension of Pacific Island
labour, and then again in large numbers after 1921 when
immigration to the United States was restricted.

North Queensland still had a reputation as the home of
fearful diseases. In the first decade of the twentieth century the
decline of mining left farming as the mainstay of north
Queensland, with a high degree of specialisation; sugar along the

coast, with maize and dairy-farming occupying the Atherton Tableland (Bolton 1963: 299–30). The Chinese began to lose their monopoly of Tableland agriculture after the Mareeba-Herberton railway was extended to Atherton in 1903. Slowly the early settlers were replaced; many Chinese left the district during World War I and the land was resumed by government for the settlement of ex-servicemen. As the sugar industry learned to do without coloured labour so the Atherton Highlands were developed as a white area with the influx of new settlers after 1907. It was the sugar industry which led to growing integration with the rest of Australia, and slowly non-European labour, including some Indian canecutters and the Japanese employees (Bolton 1963: 309), was eliminated.

North Queensland was firmly established as a 'white man's tropics' a hundred years after settlement (Bolton 1963: 323). Smallholder farming was well instituted and the system continued to appeal to migrant families from southern Europe (Bolton 1963: 325). The decay of Chinese banana plantations at Innisfail had attracted considerable numbers of Italian and Sicilian settlers during the 1920s, leading to fears Innisfail was becoming a foreign enclave. After the wounds of fascism were healed, in the 1950s more friendly local relations obtained with the Italians.

And Another Tale ...

Now let us tell another tale. At perhaps the time when Queensland gold was first reaching the ports of Hong Kong and Guangdong, attracting the first southern Chinese goldseekers to Australia, an upland tribal southern Chinese minority, the Hmong (devastated after their participation in several disastrous rebellions against the central Chinese state and in search of new lands to cultivate), slowly began to infiltrate into the mountainous uplands of the country which became part of the French colony of Indochina (Vietnam and Laos). As subsistence cultivators, and as the inhabitants of strategically important borderland regions, they were inevitably implicated in the struggle against colonial domination which was to become the Vietnam War, and which also affected large areas of neighbouring Laos. Hmong were drawn into fighting on both sides in this globalised conflict, for the communists, backed by the Soviet Union and China, and for the

Western-supported struggle against communism in both Laos and Vietnam. Again Australia was involved. For, in 1951, an educational initiative, the Colombo Plan,[1] was started with the assistance of the Southeast Asia Treaty Organisation (a strategic organisation set up to protect Southeast Asia from what was feared would be the 'domino' effects of communism in North Vietnam).

Some Hmong came to Australia under the Colombo Plan as schoolchildren at that time, part of a new breed of Southeast Asians the West hoped to encourage to fight communism. After the fall of Vietnam, and the subsequent collapse of Laos in 1975, tens of thousands of Hmong who had supported the American war effort in Laos flooded across the border into Thailand, and were settled in various refugee camps along the Thai-Lao border. From there they were resettled in many Western countries, including Australia. By 1985, 344 had settled here (Lee 1986); by 1996, the number was 1,421 (Lee 2001). Mostly they lived in Sydney, Melbourne or Hobart. The original Colombo Plan students who stayed on and who were familiar both with the situation of the Hmong back home and with Australian life, were crucial in assisting in this resettlement, advising the new arrivals, and interceding for them with the authorities.

In 1987, one daring and pioneering Hmong family went on a holiday to north Queensland from Sydney, and were attracted by stories of the profits to be made from banana plantations in the semi-tropical climate of north Queensland. They came up to Innisfail and indeed did well, leasing land and planting banana in the old sugar-cane plantations which had been worked by Italian immigrants (see also Lee, this volume). They were probably not aware that they were reviving the practices of immigrants from the same part of the world — southern China — a century before. But they will have known that in Laos, Thailand, and in Vietnam too, the Hmong often grew bananas in small plantations around the homestead and the village. Attracted by their success, many more Hmong families from Sydney moved up to Innisfail and invested in land. Some moved later to Cairns, and these north Queensland Hmong were joined in the early 1990s by other Hmong from Victoria, since which time Hmong have moved in from Hobart and elsewhere in Australia, and even New Zealand.

The Research Visit

In November 2002 I accompanied Dr Gary Lee, one of those (like Dr Pao Saykao in Melbourne, and Vw Thaow in Hobart) who had originally come to Australia under the Colombo Plan, and had subsequently been instrumental in helping many of his fellow countrymen to settle in Australia, on a research visit to Cairns and Innisfail, after a previous research visit to the Hmong community in Melbourne. This visit was funded by the Chiang Ching-Kuo Foundation in Taiwan, and formed part of a larger research project which involved the study, not only in Australia but also in Thailand, Laos and southern China, of the new transnational contacts being formed between Hmong who, after their flight from Laos, had been scattered across the continents of the world. The aim of the project was to examine the return visits of overseas Hmong to their old homes in Southeast Asia, or even to the more distant homes of their ancestors five to seven generations ago, in southern China, to see what impact these visits and their new global relationships were having on specific locations in Thailand, Laos and China. In a future extension of the project it was planned to include Vietnam, Canada, France and the United States.

By examining the economic, cultural and social transformations of localities resulting from these returns of diasporic minority migrants, the project intended to contribute to Chinese diasporic studies, which had rarely included studies of ethnic minorities, nor focused on the return visits of overseas migrants to Asian homelands. It was hoped that our research would result in a new model for the integration of local with global data, and that it might also contribute to more general debates about the romantic sources of modern individualism, the nostalgic consumption of local 'roots' as commodities, and the significance of structures of local desire in constituting transnational identities through the formation of cultural strategies by the members of new social movements, or what Werbner (1996) calls 'communal diasporic voluntary public culture'. Besides testing what we had already learned in Asia about the impact there of overseas Hmong, we had also been testing the major hypothesis that the Hmong were forming a new kind of transnational community through international visits, marriages and telecommunications such as the internet. We interviewed a large number of people, and this chapter represents some of the results of that research in Innisfail and Cairns, with some reference to comparable materials collected in Melbourne.

North Queensland

General Introduction

During our fieldwork in north Queensland, we spent most of the time in Innisfail, where there were 70 Hmong families with a total population of approximately 450. Thirty-five (now 23) of these families leased or owned plantations (mostly of banana, but some specialised in papaya, lemongrass, ginger or sweet potato for the Asian market, and there was a significant amount of poultry and pig keeping), having moved up from Sydney and elsewhere since the early 1990s.[2] Other jobs in the community ranged from Christian pastor to housing association worker, banana packer and cook in Chinese takeaways, steel welder or hired plantation labourer, and there is a low rate of unemployment compared with other Hmong communities.[3]

Cairns is the big city, and port, in this region, and Innisfail a somewhat sleepy coastal town into which the Hmong seem to have fitted without much outward difficulty. As Bolton (1963: 334) remarked, the fusion of Italian with Anglo-Irish immigrants has been so successful that one may only glimpse it in the good quality of the bread at Ingham and Innisfail, and the roving eyes of the young men as they prowl the streets of sugar towns in the evening. An elderly local resident still remembered when as many as a third of the town's population had been Italian. The Hmong live in suburban houses of varying size and status, and manage their farms in the country through daily visits.

The Hmong community in Innisfail (which had a population of 20,800 in 1996 if the surrounding rural areas of Johnston Shire are included), enjoy generally good relations with the local community, as the ex-President of the Hmong

Association (Xao Lee) explained to us. During his two-year period of office he had made efforts to contact the local council, the police, the hospital and other public agencies, about the Hmong community, and this seemed to have paid off well, for example in terms of some support received from the local council. The main points of contact for the Hmong community with the wider society were through the local Multicultural Officer, who visited regularly, and through the Mayor of Innisfail. The local population was composed of Italians, Greeks, and Indian banana farmers besides those of Anglo-Irish descent, some Macedonians and Yugoslavs, and still the remnants of the South Sea Islanders originally hired as canecutters by Irish plantation owners.

The former President stressed to us that there were bound to be some problems within the Hmong community since, as he pointed out, it is composed of the members of radically different social strata from Laos: ex-soldiers, ex-farmers, and ex-students. He saw one of his main tasks as explaining to the older members of the Hmong community the relevance of Australian laws as opposed to traditional attitudes 'like the idea that you can beat your wife, or kill her lover'.

He emphasised how few problems there were with other local farmers — the farmers all stick together, and help each other, he said. There were sometimes problems with neighbours, he admitted, particularly over the large gatherings the Hmong sometimes have for ritual or ceremonial occasions. For example, there must have been over a hundred people at a shamanic session (*ua neeb*) we attended, and the whole road was jam-packed with Hmong cars. 'I do think some parts of our culture may just not be suitable for the life here', he confessed. Sometimes there were other small problems, over kids picking fruit, for example. But the majority of people were 'okay', and the Hmong here always took pains to inform neighbours beforehand when major social events were to occur. In striking contrast to the ethnic violence and conflict which seems to have characterised the area, therefore, the Hmong today appear to live in an open and largely accepting society. Local non-Hmong residents confirmed this view of things.

Owing to the small numbers of Hmong in Australia, clan organisation does not seem to have adopted the radical forms it has

in countries where there are much greater population
concentrations, like the United States where over 180,000 Hmong
now live. Instead, local associations have been initiated which are
not exclusively clan-based and, as we were told with some pride in
Innisfail, it is customary to invite members of other clans to
weddings and ritual events, unlike what is felt to be the case in the
United States or elsewhere. American Hmong, they feel, are 'not
friendly', in the words of one informant.

Although many moved to north Queensland with clear
hopes of commercial gain, the Hmong who first settled in Innisfail
must have been the pioneers, the far-sighted yet nostalgic ones who
had not yet lost sight of their farming backgrounds in Laos, and
had hoped to revive them by moving into this region. It was by no
means everyone among the Australian Hmong who came to
Innisfail, yet those who came must have been in some way
dissatisfied with their previous urban existence (jobs reported in
Sydney ranged from making window-frames in a factory to car-
repairing) and longing, in almost a New Age way, for a more
substantial life. One old man at a shamanic session told me that
banana farming was a bit like life in Laos had been; although it was
hard work, at least your time was your own, and you could rest
when you liked. The Innisfail community is today seen as
conservative by other Hmong, particularly those from overseas
countries, and this may be a reflection of the way the Australian
Hmong are generally viewed by those of other Western countries.
One Hmong woman from France, who had moved to Melbourne
to get married, talked of her attraction and shock to discover how
'strict' and 'old-fashioned' the Hmong here were, and this she said
had given her a sense of security, a sense of 'coming home'.[4]
Certainly the need to live together in a large (*coob*) group has been
important in the many secondary relocations which have taken
place since the Hmong first arrived in Australia (and secondary
relocation of large groups has also been a phenomenon in France
and the UnitedStates). This was one of the main reasons given for
why all fifteen Hmong families settled in New Zealand had
recently moved to Innisfail, together with the lack of ritual
specialists. In one case a body had to be sent to the United States

for the proper death rites, owing to the original sons of the deceased having settled there. This scarcity of ritual specialists remains a very real problem for the Australian Hmong, who now number nearly 2,000.

The 'sucriers' or baby bananas of Indonesian origin in which they tend to specialise, I was told, are mostly sold to Asian vendors, and it was the need for these to be altar offerings for the Vietnamese in Melbourne which led to the original demand for them in that city. There are of course hundreds of strains from Laos which could be planted here, and which might sell more successfully, but in general Australian restrictions on imports of organic produce are too stringent for them to have attempted this. Other Asians besides the Hmong and Vietnamese prefer the 'Daccas' while Westerners prefer the larger Cavendish which sell in supermarkets. We visited one farm of 66 acres, the next one had 40 and that was also the size of our host's.

However, most families are now beginning to sell their farm leases off and discussing a further relocation to Brisbane or other places. Today there are Hmong communities in both Cairns (predominantly Christian Green Hmong who had arrived later in Australia) and Innisfail, and Cairns is now attracting an increasing proportion of the youth from Innisfail in search of new work opportunities, as we see below. And there are separate local Hmong associations; the Innisfail-based North Queensland Hmong Association, affiliated to the national organisation of the Hmong Australia Society (see Lee, in this volume), which includes members of the cultural Hmong Federation based in Cairns as well as the SPK housing association there, but not of a break-away Hmong Council also based in Innisfail.[5]

Data on Return Visits

Exogamous patrilineal clans are pivotal in Hmong social organisation, and in the following I consider population figures according to their breakdown by membership of different clans (Xyooj, Tsab, Yaj, and so on).[6] In Cairns, at the time we visited, there were seventeen of the Xyooj clan in three families, 106 of the Tsab in sixteen families, 41 Yaj in seven families, 14 Lis in two households, 15 Hawj in two, 18 Kwm in three, 24 Vaj in four households, eight Muas in just one family, 32 Vwj in three families, and 28 Thoj in five families; that is, a population of 303, in 47 households. Household size ranged from two to eleven, with an average of 6.4. In Innisfail (excluding approximately 87 Hmong Council members — some 40 adults — for whom this information was not available), there were 56 of the Vwj clan in eight families, 40 Lis in six households, 25 Xyooj in four households, 16 Lauj in three, three Muas in one household, 96 Vaj in twelve households (although one of these was headed by an inmarrying Cambodian male), and 93 Yaj in fifteen households; that is, a population of 360, in 49 households. Household size also ranged from two to eleven, and the average household size was 7.3.[7]

The cases of returnees to Laos and visitors to other countries which I give below, covered the total Innisfail Hmong population, including the Hmong Council members excluded from the figures above.

The data collected from Innisfail on returns to Laos was extremely accurate and meaningful and can in my opinion very probably be generalised to other Hmong communities in Australia, although it must be recognised that it represents the *maximum* extent of contacts with the homeland to be found in any Hmong community in Australia; that is, there were more contacts with the homeland here than there would be among any other Hmong communities in Australia. From that data, including Hmong Council members, out of exactly 134 adults of over eighteen years of age in Innisfail, only 31 had been back to Laos at all. This percentage (23.1 per cent) would of course diminish considerably if we considered it against the total Hmong population in Innisfail of 450, and would diminish even further in other locations in Australia. But it is surely significant that as many as nineteen out of these 31 visitors (over half of them) had not only visited Laos, but had also made visits to Hmong communities in the United States, while in addition to the 31 who had revisited Laos, a further 28 had visited the United States without undertaking any visits to Laos at all. In other words, an overall total of 59 adults, or nearly half the total adult population of 134, had undertaken overseas visits to Laos or America. And visitors to the United States (47 altogether) well outnumbered those to Laos (31). The figures are even clearer when one considers the number of total visits made, since often more than one visit was made; the total number of *visits* to the United States, as against visitors, was 66, whereas only 38 visits altogether had been made to Laos.

To anticipate our conclusions, it did seem, from both this and other evidence, that more linkages are being formed between Hmong in First World countries than are being formed between First World and Third World Hmong, and that, as we show below, rather than any single or unitary Hmong community emerging internationally, through modern communications and transport, a number of very different appeals are being made to that imagined sense of unity.

Ages of visitors to Laos were almost invariably over 40; only five out of the 31 were under 40 years of age. The 31 cases of adult Innisfail Hmong who had been back to Laos includes nine wives who had been accompanying their husbands, and one divorced couple who had both been back to Laos separately to remarry (we met the second wife of the man later in Cairns at Rusty's Market, where several Hmong women make a good living selling fresh fruit and vegetables). They also include a mother and daughter who had visited together, and the sister of one of the nine wives who had accompanied her and her husband, all for medical reasons. Two out of the nine couples had travelled together making up a group of four, and one other woman (a friend) had accompanied one of the couples. None of these visitors had taken their children back to Laos, but two of those who had also visited the United States had once taken their children there with them.

Four of the Laos returnees had made two visits; so had the mother whose daughter had accompanied her on one of these visits, as had the wife whose sister had accompanied her referred to above, and also the divorced wife also referred to above. Of the first four who had revisited Laos twice (which was the most times anyone had been back), one had been looking for a wife in Laos, and had also visited the United States, one had been looking for a wife in Laos, and had also visited France; another had also been looking for a wife in Laos, but had not been to any other countries, while the last case had also visited the United States, but had not been in search of a wife. The mother whose daughter had accompanied her (on one of her two visits to Laos) had also visited the United States; so had the wife whose sister had accompanied her once, and who had adopted a child in the United States (see below); and so also had the divorced wife who was in search of a new husband. Out of the nineteen of these visitors to Laos who had also made visits to the United States, two had made two visits to the United States, and three had made three or more visits to the United States (including the couple who adopted the American child). Out of the 31 who had revisited Laos, fourteen in all were women (including the nine accompanying wives, the divorced wife, the mother and daughter, the sister of the adopting couple, and the friend of the accompanying wife).

Of the 28 cases who had visited the United States, but had made no return visits back to Laos or Thailand, nine of these were also wives accompanying their husbands — although one of these accompanying wives had originally come from the States — and there were four other married women who had been to the United States without their spouses; one to see close relatives, one to see her parents, one to see her daughter. At least four of these cases had taken their children with them to the United States; four children in three cases, one daughter in the other. Four out of the 28 had made two visits to the States, one had been there three times, and one had been four times (the husband of the woman who had made three visits). The wives of three of the four men who had made two visits to the United States had only visited there once (including the wife who had originally come from the States). Ages of these United States visitors were not collected.

Apart from the divorced couple, who had both found new spouses in Laos, two of those who had revisited Laos had successfully found wives there — both of these were among those who had visited Laos twice, and one was the one who had also visited France (the only case of a visit to France in Innisfail). I have mentioned above the other case of a man who had been to the United States twice, but not to Laos at all, and whose wife came from the United States.[8]

Reasons for Returns

The explicit reasons for return visits to Laos varied widely; apart from the elderly divorced couple referred to above, who both contracted successful marriages with Hmong from Laos, three other men had gone back to Laos explicitly to find a wife. One shaman had revisited 'for cultural reasons'. The most common specific explanation was 'medical' in nature; the mother and daughter pair referred to above had been back for medical reasons (*kho mob*), as had another couple. The two couples who had travelled in a group together had all gone for medical reasons, and so had the wife and her friend who had accompanied her and her husband (that is, a man went back with his wife and his wife's friend who were both travelling for medical reasons). One of the other couples who revisited had also done so for specific medical reasons to do with fertility; it is quite often the case that couples who are unable to bear children may feel that only a special shamanic session in Laos or Thailand may help them, or particular types of herbal medicine (*tshuaj ntsuab*) which can only be obtained there. In my travels around Thailand the previous year with a visiting Hmong couple from the United States, medical reasons had played a part in their visit; they had particularly wished to consult a certain shaman who lived in the north of Thailand, and showed a great interest in various herbs and spices which we found in Hmong villages along the Lao border.

In one very sad case among the above revisiting couples from Innisfail, the sister of one wife who had accompanied her and her husband on one of their visits had done so specifically because her sister was unable to have a child, and this was also the reason for the couple's visit. This couple had also visited the United States several times (the husband had accompanied his wife three times, and she had made two further visits alone), in order to adopt her sister's child from the United States (her sister was settled in the United States), having failed after a number of tragic years in their efforts to adopt a child from another country. This adopting couple was a very special case, and yet in their story one can see something of the way Hmong *kinship* relations (see below) can often work to support individuals in difficulties across the oceans.

They had spent years trying to adopt a child since their first arrival in Australia in 1979. Her own parents had been resettled in the United States, together with her two sisters and two brothers, where her mother had remarried, so that effectively all her own nearest relatives were in the United States.

In 1986 she and her husband had visited Korea with the intention of adopting a child but were finally refused, she said, both because they were classified as 'animists' rather than belonging to a 'proper' religion, and because she could produce no Australian Higher Education Certificate (how could she have done?). It was too difficult to arrange an adoption from China, and Taiwan was also ruled out because they were not Christian (she refused to convert simply in order to make adoption easier, she said). So her younger sister, in the United States, who had already had some children, 'got pregnant for me', but then she had miscarried.

Then, in 1996, this American Hmong sister 'had my son for me again', she said (using the name of her current, adopted son, referring implicitly to the Hmong belief that repeated miscarriages are caused by the playful returns of one naughty or wilful child). They had both gone over to the States for the birth, but had then had to return again to Australia after a month, and had finally managed (after another visit to the States by herself) to bring him in here as her nephew, although in Hmong eyes this was clearly a son she had adopted.

She told us the sister had 'had the child for her the second time' because her eyes kept streaming in a strange way for three months and finally she had exclaimed (to an unspecified deity) 'If you want me to have this baby, stop my eyes streaming!' — and the streaming had suddenly and inexplicably stopped. Her sister had still missed the child terribly, she said. The boy turned out to suffer from a mild autistic condition, and it was this which had led to their subsequent visits to Laos to find a shamanic or herbal cure for his condition (which was now finally improving). There are of course no formal arrangements between Australia and the United States for individual adoptions of this kind, so that now her boy was approaching school age it was imperative to formalise the adoption, and this was proving to be a legal nightmare. Their banana farm had been sold and they were considering relocation to the city with her son's future education in mind. This was a very special, and sad case, and the reason for repeating it here is that it makes the point (as Dr Pao Saykao in Melbourne had also stressed to us) that most people have very specific reasons of their own for going back to Laos or Thailand, and the case also underlines the importance of these so very recently severed kinship ties across the globe (see below).

Besides 'medical reasons' of various kinds, the other main reason given for revisits to Laos was in order to see relatives. Probably every case in the 31 had visited relatives of close or near distance during their revisits to Laos or Thailand, but two cases had gone specifically to see relatives for particular reasons, another had been back to see his mother when she became very ill, and another specifically to see his parents who had been repatriated back to Laos from Thailand in about 1995. Reasons were, therefore, quite specific and personal, and overwhelmingly linked with family and kinship (see below, *The Importance of Kinship*). For example, one man from Cairns had revisited Thailand in order to assist in the wedding of a classificatory nephew to a local Hmong girl (originally from Laos) whose parents were demanding an outrageously high wedding payment of some one hundred thousand *baht*.[9]

In our previous research in Asia, on the local impact there of Hmong who were visiting from overseas locations (such as Australia), we had found a variety of motivations besides simple nostalgia given for these visits. For example, in Wenshan prefecture of China, close to the Vietnam border, which is regularly visited by overseas Hmong (overwhelmingly from the United States, as was the case in all the Asian locations we visited), five broad categories of overseas Hmong visitors had emerged from our interviews with local Hmong, and with those who were visiting from overseas; the most important and primary reason given for return visits was the wish to visit relatives or to discover family links and original places. This probably plays a primary part in almost all overseas Hmong revisits to Asian locations. But in addition to those who visited primarily for reasons to do with kinship, there were also those who came back 'for business reasons'; with hopes or plans of establishing international business and trading relations through local Hmong links.

Other categories of visitors included: religious missionaries, since there are quite a number of Protestant Hmong in the United States attached to various churches who revisit for the purposes of proselytisation, some Catholics or members of other religious organisations; and also political emissaries, those in the cause of General Vang Pao, the retired Hmong General from Laos now resident in the United States, who supports and sponsors factions of an ongoing Hmong resistance in Laos. Finally, very commonly among the overseas visitors have been those who are in search of love, or second wives, sometimes after divorces overseas, sometimes by those who are already married (since traditional Hmong culture allows second marriages by men). Local reactions were very mixed towards these overseas Hmong, whom some Hmong in Australia (and Thailand and China) said tended to be those who had not adjusted well to their new lives overseas, were out of work and going back to impress, and serious local problems had emerged regarding all these categories of overseas Hmong visitor except the first (the ones who visited purely for family reasons). It was the last ('love') category, where problems seemed to have been most acute and were most discussed. It is quite common, for example, for Hmong men from overseas to revisit Thailand, Laos or even China at the Hmong New Year, and to start a local affair with a Hmong (or in some cases Chinese) girl, which they have no intention of formalising into a marriage, perhaps because they already have a wife overseas who knows nothing about it, and there are many stories of these kinds of deceptions and a certain amount of local anger about it.

Some of these more regular visitors, particularly from the United States and France, keep effective concubines in Asian locations whom they visit regularly and provide some support to. 'Hmong men just go back for fun,' said one teenage informant in Melbourne dismissively. On the other hand, this kind of liaison cannot occur without some local complicity. When I visited the

Hmong settlement in Thailand where the high bridewealth case referred to above occurred, local Hmong leaders told me that people were generally wise now to these sorts of tricks (and this was why high wedding payments were sometimes demanded when an overseas Hmong offered to marry a local girl), but some of the young girls just did not care if they were exploited, they said; they just went with visiting American Hmong for the sake of money or other benefits, not expecting marriage or a permanent liaison, and would not listen to the injunctions of their parents and elders! This was a different kind of youth recalcitrance from that of the young Hmong people in Australia in their wholesale rejection of, or disinterest in, Hmong cultural traditions (see below), but similarly distressing for their parents.

Overseas Marriages

A number of international marriages had taken place, although less in Cairns/Innisfail than in Melbourne, some of these based on previous contacts through the internet. In Melbourne we had interviewed members of one somewhat extraordinary family with one brother in France and one in the United States who maintained extensive contacts through visits and a dedicated family web page and information bulletin. Two brothers, who lived together with two other brothers in a large extended family in Melbourne, had married Hmong girls from France, while a third had had extensive internet relationships with girls from overseas. As the latter put it to us, he had been twice to the United States to visit girls, each time a different one, and one American Hmong girl had come here specifically to visit him. In each case he had chatted online with them and exchanged emails with them for periods of time ranging from several years to six months to a brief exchange of emails before their actual meetings had taken place. He said he had also had some real-life romances in Australia, but was very gloomy about the chances of finding a wife here. He complained that the 'supply' of girls here was too small, and there were none older than 21. 'The girls are dying out!' he exclaimed. Of course, his assumption was that he should find a Hmong mate, and this we found to be a very general one. Besides these cases, one (Thoj) girl had gone to the United States to find a husband and had settled there, one American girl had visited and married (a Xyooj) here, one (Yaj) man had found a wife from Fresno, and there was one case of a wife being found from Laos after divorce.

In Innisfail there had been three cases among those we recorded of men who had gone back to Laos/Thailand explicitly to find wives, besides the divorced wife who had found a new husband there, and the case of the nephew in Cairns noted above. Apart from the case of the visitor to the United States whose wife had come from the States, one other girl in Innisfail had also married there (Tooj Xeeb Yaj's daughter). A further three girls had married Australians, and one girl had gone off to Ireland with a backpacker she had met locally and married. Despite a general disinterest in Hmong culture and history among Hmong raised in Australia, or under 40 years of age, which we examine in more detail below, the preference is still very much to marry Hmong spouses. We were told that it was relatively common for a boyfriend or girlfriend to be an Australian, but marriages were overwhelmingly with other Hmong.

The girls we interviewed were understandably somewhat circumspect about their use of the internet to find potential marriage partners. 'We are aware of the Hmong in other places,' said one, delicately. In practice, however, these are as likely — if not more likely — to be in New South Wales or Hobart as overseas. 'There are so few Hmong here,' said one teenager, 'most girls are looking for Hmong lovers on the internet and wanting to go to the US.'

It seems that while the internet is used as a means of meeting other Hmong, not only overseas but also across Australia, by the younger people and teenagers, where international marriages do take place, they may generally tend to strengthen Hmong custom and tradition. One informant in Melbourne, for example, had married a Hmong from France, whom he had met here, whose parents had subsequently been unable to join them in Australia; at the time they married, his Hmong was falling away as he was more used to speaking in English, while her French was very much better than her Hmong. Now, however, they usually speak Hmong to each other.

In another interesting case there, a young schoolgirl who had just begun to enjoy the internet and was speaking English better than Hmong, had been married off reluctantly at a very young age to a much older man from France, but had since then become an explicitly contented, fairly traditional Hmong wife. 'I am an innocent girl and my husband is much older and knows many things so I have to trust him and look up to him and obey him. To start with I was quite angry but after I knew his family and relations it was better. You have to get to know someone ... *nws paub lus*' (literally, 'he understands [peoples'] words', or 'he knows stuff', that is, is mature). The few international marriages there had been seemed therefore to play some part in maintaining Hmong cultural traditions which were otherwise dramatically weakening.

Internet usage, however, had had to stop with her marriage. Recently there has been much talk about the terrible case of Pa Shia, a well educated young Hmong wife in California who spent so much time on the internet that her husband became jealous and tried to stop her. 'Only if you kill me will I shut up,' she is alleged to have said, so he did shoot her, and himself, and their children (he survived; see discussion on Hmong Social Cultural Group 2000).

There seems less interest in Innisfail than in Melbourne in finding spouses overseas or using the internet for that purpose, and one cannot help wondering whether this may be related in some way to the high rate of visits back to Southeast Asia among the north Queensland Hmong by comparison to other Hmong communities elsewhere in Australia.

The Importance of Kinship

Reasons connected with recently severed kinship ties have been fundamental in bringing Hmong visitors back to Laos and Thailand, and even in visiting other Hmong communities in the United States, where almost every Hmong in the community has at least one close relative, and we have seen something of the strength of close family ties across divided continents in the case of the child adopted from the sister described above. The important role played by kinship in the global ties now being formed between the diasporic Hmong community was impressed on us in a number of ways. One Innisfail family showed us a questionnaire entitled the 'United Yang Family Survey 2000'. The survey had been prepared in the United States, and is being distributed among all Hmong members of the Yang clan globally. It asks for information (in Hmong and English) on religion (old or new) and leadership experience (*kev coj noj coj ua*) besides educational level, occupation, and details of wife and children. On the back of the form there is a skeleton genealogical diagram for ego's generation and four ascending paternal generations, and the brothers and sisters of each, with the names left blank to be filled in. Here an appeal to Hmong global unity was certainly been made, but purely on a clan basis.

In the huge house of one banana farmer, whose wife's brother also has a plantation, we were told how he worked hard from dawn to well past dusk every day on his 70 acres and how the price of bananas had fallen from 25 dollars to 15 per carton since 1995-96, when they had moved up from Sydney, where he had been working in a factory making picture-frames. He was now thinking of selling up. With relatives still in Laos and a brother still in Wat Tam Krabok (the famous Buddhist temple in Thailand which houses many Hmong refugees from Laos), an incredible family reunion had taken place earlier in the year. His sister, whom he had not seen for two decades, came from France, together with the husband she had married in Thailand but whom he had never met, and their children. His mother's sister had come from France, as well as his father, who had exited Laos later than he had and was now settled in the States with a new wife, and also his mother, who now lived with her brother in Sydney, and a married sister from Sydney, making up a joyous party of ten. This informant was one of those who had visited the States together with his children since, as he said, his main motive for the visit was to have his children know their cousins and other relatives there. He had also been back to Laos with another couple and his wife who had a bad back, where he had visited a famous shaman. However, the visit to Laos had not gone well; they had only been allowed five days there and had had to bribe the local police for that. One of the reasons why more visits to the United States may be occurring is the practical difficulties for many Hmong, particularly those blacklisted as previous reactionaries, of getting into Laos at all. But these sorts of reunions of globally dispersed families can only rarely happen.

The primordial importance of kinship in the visits Hmong make back to homelands as well as to new Hmong communities in other First World countries, and as perhaps the major factor unifying the globally scattered Hmong, was much impressed upon us through this visit. One key informant in Melbourne had remarked how he thought the Hmong already had virtual families, and that now they needed to establish a global virtual community. The internet is of course one key way in which to do that, and although its use and frequency was less than we had expected when beginning this project (since many families do not have internet access nor the ability to use computers), it did seem that it might be fulfilling something of the same functions as the kinship system did when the Hmong were divided from each other through their traditional lives as shifting cultivators.

Economic and Other Relations Overseas

Almost all of those who still had relatives in Laos or Thailand supported them financially. It is difficult to obtain accurate figures of these very personal payments among different families, but our research in Thailand and Laos, and also China, had already alerted us to its significance and given us some idea of its extent. In Innisfail informants estimated the average sent back by particular families in Laos or Thailand annually was around the A$500 mark. One ritual specialist told us of his two sisters in Laos whom he had supported regularly for a number of years. He planned to return to Laos next year specifically to help his sister build a house which he thought might cost the equivalent of US$9,000 in all. He calculated he sent as much as A$3,000 a year back home, in small amounts of a few hundred a time. Another informant sent about A$400–500 each year, to both Laos and Thailand but predominantly to Laos, especially at the New Year. His wife and children also helped relatives from Laos, now in Thailand, sell *paj ntaub* (Hmong traditional embroideries) for them and sent back perhaps A$700–800 each year to them. We were told that almost everyone, or at least 90 per cent of the community (meaning household heads) sent something back to relatives in Laos or Thailand, ranging from A$500 to A$3,000 in any single month, usually in small batches of hundreds and mostly for specific occasions, such as a funeral, sickness, the repair of a house, or the New Year.

Besides these regular remittances sent back home or to relatives in Thailand, which are a constant drain on the resources of newly arrived displaced persons and recently resettled families, but have a far-reaching impact on local communities in China and Laos as we have witnessed, other economic relations with Hmong overseas were in general less than we had expected, although they do exist and they are important.

One Innisfail man with family in Sydney, Brisbane and Canberra, had a part-share with another family member of a grocery-cum-boutique store in St Paul, Minnesota, managed by affinal relatives there. This was a properly run and genuinely international business involving buyers from the United States visiting Thailand and international taxation agreements.[10] Yet these enterprises are very much the exception, and most overseas contacts of an economic nature are likely to be through the small-scale family-based traditional costumes industry, with relatives in Thailand sending products which may be finished overseas and sold elsewhere, through the circulation of Hmong videos, produced by American Hmong often in Southeast Asian locations with local Hmong assistance, which occupy the nostalgia and time of the elderly, or through remittances sent back to relatives in Laos. Other contacts overseas included, for example, fairly extensive visits made by a Christian pastor in Melbourne for training courses in Thailand, and regular visits to him by American pastors of the Christian Alliance Church (see www.hmongdistrict.org) and the housing association in Cairns planned to link up shortly with overseas Hmong organisations.

Dissatisfaction Among Youth

It may fairly be said that the Hmong are in cultural crisis, with the elders alarmed at the loss of Hmong culture by the youth, and some of the young men in Melbourne very concerned about the lack of eligible Hmong spouses who tend to marry early. Many of our informants feared or felt that the Hmong would 'disappear' (*ploj*) as a people within a generation if these trends continued.

The attempt to revive a traditional agrarian life in Innisfail has not, overall, been a success. Banana prices have fallen owing, it was said, largely to the increasing numbers of people joining the business and the rising prices of chemicals and diesel fuel. On the roads we saw bananas advertised at one dollar per kilogram-bunch, but we were told a 13-kilogram carton had previously fetched up to sixty dollars in Melbourne. There was general agreement that the children hated to come to the farms, feeling that farmwork is too 'dirty', and there are few work opportunities locally for the younger generation. The younger generation are, inevitably, dissatisfied, as it is said those who had been resettled in French Guyana and successfully adopted a farming life are, and now many of the banana farmers are talking of selling up and moving to Brisbane. There has been regular annual movement of families to Cairns as children left Year 12 of schooling to find work in town.

Many of the younger Hmong feel only a faint curiosity towards their own backgrounds and cultural heritage. One 16-year old girl said of Hmong custom and tradition, 'my view is we won't need it, when we go into the real world'. As she said, she was 'not very interested in Hmong culture', but liked softball and netball. 'My Hmong now is not too good,' said an 18-year old TAFE college student, 'you probably need to understand the culture, to speak the language ... *Kevcai* — probably very interesting ...' Another married man of 30 with young children complained that with both he and his wife working and the children at the Day Care Centre all day they had almost no chance to speak Hmong with them, so the children knew no Hmong. He had no feelings at all about going back to visit Laos, and didn't know how he would *cope* there with no toilets or clean water to drink or shops down the road. His family had no religion, he said, but just followed his father who was a ritual expert. If his kids wanted to learn about it, he said, they could ask their grandfather who they saw every weekend or so. 'Sure — Hmong *kevcai* [customs] will disappear. I don't have any knowledge of it, and I won't force my children to learn it. I choose not to know about it — so it will die! If you believe it, it must matter I guess. It's too late for me to learn about it, or want to learn about it, and I don't have much interest in wanting to learn about it. From what I understand, funerals are the most important *kevcai*, and I just want there still to be *kevcai* so when my father dies he can have that, but after that I don't mind.'

Those of the older generation are sufficiently concerned about this lack of cultural competence among the youth to have started a variety of cultural transmission attempts, and there are now active attempts to keep Hmong culture alive by teaching it to younger people in centres in many different countries, including Thailand. In Melbourne we had visited one centre where 15–20 men, none too young, were learning the Song of Opening the Way which is sung at a death (*qhuab ke*), how to call the soul (*hu plig*), and perform ancestral domestic worship (*ua dab xwm kab*) and the wedding songs (*zaj tshoob*), and another informant organised his own regular sessions at his home. Attendance seemed fairly desultory and there was an air of artificiality about these places; but it must be remembered that these traditional skills and competences would normally have been passed from a parent to a child, or from a Master to a disciple, and their transmission in the public arena marks a real sign of concern about the perceived loss of cultural heritage and a real recognition of the efforts needed to maintain it.

Messianism and Nationalism

There is also one tendency which continues this desire to resuscitate traditional Hmong culture in a bizarre form disliked by almost all the local Hmong. The original pioneer, who had moved up to Innisfail from Sydney to initiate the first Hmong banana plantation, had squandered his new-found wealth through various means, lost his land and was then reduced to watching other Hmong, who had followed his example and moved up to Innisfail, making good where, it seemed, he himself had failed. After an abortive attempt to immigrate to the United States, and a venture into the restaurant business, he became a member of a new religious cult founded by a member of another clan who had unsuccessfully struggled with the local pastor for control of the Hmong Christian community (see also Wronska-Friend, this volume).

This novel religious movement has now established a temple and a priesthood, has created new syncretic beliefs and rituals (including Christian-like prayers before meals, water-sprinkling before visitors enter their houses after the fashion of Buddhist monks, and bowing in Japanese fashion before making offerings) and is applying for government funding under the name of the Amu. This is a composite name based on readings about other Miao groups related to the Hmong in China known as the A Hmao and the Hmu, which the cult adopted after local Hmong refused to allow them to use the name of 'Hmong' to represent their beliefs. Their ritual leader (the ex-Christian) is also a (self-taught) shaman, although the shamanism he practices is said to be very strange and unlike that of others. The cult is fire-walled by ritual beliefs in pollution and fear of contamination by the 'earthly' world, particularly by those Hmong who do not support them. It is said that the pioneer joined up with this movement after reading a book published by a local canecutter who claimed to have been taken on an extraterrestrial voyage in a UFO where he had met the Hmong well before they had arrived in Innisfail.

The sect claims to hold the secrets to a variety of world mysteries, such as the pyramids and Stonehenge, and allows intermarriage between members of different patrilineal clans. This is a Hmong, but also a New Age spiritualist movement, and its members talk easily about auras and astral bodies in true 'Madame Besant' style. They retreated from the rest of the Hmong community before the year 2000 when various floods and disasters were promised, equipped with stockpiles of rice and petrol. In common with other historic Hmong movements of resistance against established authority it is messianic; that is, it believes that a saviour will be (in fact, now has) been born who will become the Emperor of the Hmong and lead his chosen people to salvation. The ten members of this cult (four families from Innisfail, including two who had previously been members of a Chinese vegetarian cult) have retreated to the Atherton Tablelands, some 2,000 feet above sea level, rich dairy country and the site of remote early cattle stations, where they practice a modified form of vegetarianism and wear a rather remarkable form of traditional Hmong costume.

We interviewed members of this small New Age community in Atherton, all of whom, I was told, are on welfare

payments. The cult leaders have close relations with a Hmong
messianic movement originally started by Yaj Soob Lwj, which
flourished in the refugee camps along the Thai border and
supports the 'Chao Fa' resistance leaders in their doomed battle
against the Pathet Lao authorities. There are frequent visits to
Thailand to consult members of this movement and it may be
seen, therefore, as a global as well as a local response to cultural
pressures upon the Hmong community. One Hmong in
Melbourne said that he had received a telephone inquiry from
some Hmong in China who wished to know if the rumours that a
Hmong King had been born in Australia were true since they
feared the Chinese government would try to assassinate him!

Although this movement is an embarrassment to most
right-thinking Hmong (who wish the Hmong to move forward in
their history, see the movement as a regression and its leaders as
those who have failed to adjust to their new lives in the West, and
would probably prefer it not to be written about), I see it as an
important minority attempt to retain a form of traditional culture
which most Australian Hmong are, inevitably, losing. The fact that
it is not traditional culture at all, but a new form of custom and
belief, is in itself an important (and creative) response to almost
overwhelming cultural pressures to assimilate and acculturate. It is
a kind of refusal to acculturate, and an attempt to impose a form of
minority culture on the Australian consciousness in the only way
that our society is prepared to tolerate radical cultural differences
— as a fringe religious cult.

Although the movement is so small, and cannot therefore
be taken as representative of general trends among the Hmong
community in Australia, such attempts to cling to or revive
traditional culture are not confined to this movement alone nor are
they the preserve of an older generation which has found it
difficult to adjust to the life overseas. This was shown in the case of
one young man we met who has invented a new Hmong national
flag along traditional symbolic lines and told us that he wishes to
create a new movement for the global Hmong 'which will bring
Hmong together from all the different countries' based on his own
creative combinations of the history of the Hmong contained in

funeral and wedding rituals. This flag is divided into three parts by a chevron on the left side, pointing outwards towards the right. Inside the chevron it is coloured green. From the point of the chevron runs a horizontal line dividing the remainder of the flag, on its right side, into an upper and a lower half. The upper half is coloured red and says 'Xob' (the name of the Thunder God in Hmong); the lower half is blue and says 'Zaj' (which means 'Dragon', and there are many Hmong stories about the Dragon King). In the middle of the bit on the left, inside the chevron, there is a sort of a sun in the form of a smiling face with two eyes, surrounded by stars. This attempt at representing a Hmong national consciousness by a member of the younger generation is similar to the web statement, with another newly designed Hmong flag, put up by a young Hmong college student in the United States, which I have reported on elsewhere (Tapp 2003).

In Melbourne we had interviewed a shamaness whose son (whom we also interviewed) was a follower of the Chao Fa resistance messianic movement in Laos and Thailand. Another follower we interviewed had erected a substantial plaque in the same style as that pioneered by this movement, with local government assistance, which had then been vandalised. Our informants on these movements ranged from ex-soldiers (many of whom had no time for the religious aspects of the Chao Fa movement) to teenagers, and included women as well as men. Without a doubt these are minority efforts and are far from representative of the great and overwhelming majority of Hmong settlers overseas — well, let us say it clearly, they are *un*representative. Yet that they should occur at all, when considered in the light of the younger generation's very general loss of interest in or commitment to Hmong tradition, and explicit attempts all over the world, from California to Thailand as well as in Cairns, Sydney and Melbourne, to inculcate the younger generation with Hmong values, Hmong traditions and Hmong customs, is I think deeply significant and indicative of a genuine cultural crisis among the Hmong community.

Internet Usage

In terms of one of the original project goals, to contribute a model linking and integrating local with global data, the aspect of our project which concerned internet usage by the Hmong has been particularly important. The aim has been to map Hmong connections on the internet and World Wide Web, to conduct interviews with those who have produced and used them, and those who have not, and to pay particular attention to the role of electronic mail and online chat shows, and where appropriate computer role games and video conferencing, in knitting together a divided and fragmented community who have dispersed to the four quarters of the globe.

Before our fieldwork in Australia, it was already clear that internet/computer usage, while significant in most Asian field sites, had not been extensive in any of them, while in Australia internet usage proved predictably to be far more extensive than in the Asian sites. Internet usage thus related directly to the developmental profile of the nation-state concerned; it was least developed among the Hmong in China, significant but often covert and not widespread in Laos and Vietnam, rapidly expanding in Thailand and very well established in Australia as, we imagine, in other First World countries — with the probable exception of France. Similarly to return visits by the Hmong to homelands in Laos and Thailand, then, internet usage represents only a small proportion of the population, and yet it has clearly had a significant impact on the evolution and maintenance of international relations and the initiation of new contacts among the Hmong.

It did seem from our interviews in both Melbourne and Cairns, that what may be more important than relations established through the internet between Asian homelands and First World countries, is relations between Hmong in those First World countries themselves; in other words, the internet and other new means of communication may be far more prominent in forging new relations and re-attaching connections between Hmong communities in France, the United States and Australia than between those in these countries and in Asia. The regional limitations of this project forbid further extensive inquiry into this or verification; however, the Australian data went some way towards suggesting that this may be the case. While there were internet contacts with Hmong in China, in some cases followed by visits to China, and a few with Hmong in Laos and Thailand, the overwhelming majority of internet contacts took place with other Australian, or American Hmong.

The mapping of Hmong connections on the web and internet proved more difficult than anticipated and was mainly accomplished through the use of research assistants in Australia (after the use of ASTRA programming to map the major Hmong web sites and the relations between them), and an analysis of the 25 most popular Hmong web sites and online forms based on votes coming into the list, supplemented by interviewing with users and webmasters.[11]

Interviews with young people and elders about internet usage showed fairly extensive use by both teenage and young adult men and women of the internet and email and chat-rooms, but only some of this was Hmong-related and little of it related to the Hmong in Asia. Interviews with webmasters and technical pioneers illuminated something of the way the Hmong internet began and has become by now extremely well established. For example, one webmaster in Melbourne said that he had been originally directly inspired by the idealism of John Naisbitt's book (1995), *Global Paradox*, and its McLuhanesque argument that we are moving to new world of tribalism precipitated by the internet in which nation-states would become irrelevant. A relative of his at Monash University had started Laonet, a news-oriented Lao website, and with the help of another relative at the Royal Melbourne Institute of Technology, who had supplied him with a high-speed connection, he had then joined Laonet himself and searched for specific information on the Hmong. In the initial phases, considerable assistance was received by the Hmong in Australia from American webmasters, mostly college students, such as Craig Rice of the Hmong Homepage, who had pioneered Hmong sites in the United States, in just the same way as, now, Thai Hmong are requesting assistance with setting up websites from these Australian Hmong.

In this way, and originally with the use of a hand-held scanner, the Hmong Australia Resource Page website was born, and later a discussion group (the Hmong Language Users Group, or HLUG) through an internet service provider a friend had established, which they now run free through Yahoo. Instrumental in these activities has been a group of intermediary migrants who had arrived in Australia prior to the refugee exodus from Laos. This group of highly educated middle-aged Hmong, less involved in the wars of Laos than their compatriots, have been uniquely well positioned to undertake this sort of activity, since they are neither of the generation of older fighters who experienced defeat and exile from Laos, nor of the younger educated generation of Australian Hmong who are less in touch with their cultural backgrounds.

A larger research question, or hypothesis, informed our internet inquiries and the fieldwork related to this; does usage of the web and internet by Hmong in different countries to contact each other signify the forging of a genuinely globalised *communal diasporic voluntary public culture* identity for the Hmong, or should we regard these attempts as limited, fragmentary, partial and virtual attempts to resurrect a sense of community unity which has in fact been irrevocably fragmented by global dispersal — imaginary or fantasmic attempts, that is, to compensate for *de facto* social fragmentation? There are philosophical issues here which may be irresolvable, and which reflect debates on the role of art and ideology in relation to society. Mimetic reflection, or means of imaginative transcendence?

On the basis of the data we have collected (and continue to collect), we are now in a good position to shed some light on this general question, at least with regard to the Hmong global community. For example, it appears to us (although fuller confirmation of this would require further fieldwork in the United States and France), that hegemonic American Hmong voices are only partly dominating the internet (but see Julian, this volume); in fact a wide diversity of Hmong voices are speaking through these media, as can be seen in the furious arguments which have taken place on the Hmong internet about, for example, gender and religion. The fieldwork in Australia together with the results of our internet-based inquiries mainly confirmed results which had become apparent from earlier research in Thailand on similar issues, which suggested that a whole range of different kinds of appeal (Christian, conservative, rationalist, and so on) are being made to the supposed global unity of Hmong society. In one example of this, the group of messianic Hmong who use a particular mystic script for writing the Hmong language (for which fonts have now been made available on the Web; see http://hmong.scriptmania.com/phistory.htm) had recently approached HLUG for permission to use their script in discussions through HLUG. After extensive debate this was allowed, but with the proviso that the romanised alphabet generally used for Hmong (RPA) should remain the main medium of communication. In this way one can see how the Hmong parts of the internet and world wide web in fact function to reflect real schisms and divisions of a society rather than function to overcome or transcend them; a vital mirror of the social worlds, in which conflicts are played out and moral choices must be made (like attitudes towards the Amu movement, or the breakaway Hmong Council) which themselves express wider issues of cultural liberality and tolerance and definition.

Conclusions and Discussion

This research project was originally based on the assumption of major economic transformations of Asian homelands as a result of return migrant visits, and the use of the internet in facilitating the emergence of a new form of global voluntary public diasporic culture. However, it has revealed the internet more as a reflection of society than as a means of transcending social forces; the diversity of the Hmong community apparent in the real world is only too clearly reflected on the internet. While many appeals to a global Hmong unity are made, on the internet as in political and cultural life in reality, these emanate from different groups within the Hmong community and are often at odds with each other. Reverse migration and tourism to Asian locations have certainly taken place, but only among a small minority of the older overseas population, and while these encounters have led to new international linkages and alliances, in each particular national location, social, political and economic forces have acted as severe constraints and brakes on the emergence of a genuinely diasporic community. At the same time, while Asian locations have not been substantially transformed as a result of these visits, their impact and the impact of the financial support which Asian Hmong receive from overseas Hmong has been significant in transforming Hmong perceptions of the outside world, leading to transformations of the Hmong cultural heritage and outlook at the local level.

In Australia, as also we hypothesise in other First World locations, the trend towards assimilation and loss of the Hmong identity is overpowering, particularly among the younger generation whose command of the Hmong language and knowledge of traditional Hmong customs is a source of continuing concern to the older generation. Where transnational marriages do take place, they tend to reverse this trend; thus an Australian Hmong, with better English language skills than Hmong language skills, marrying a French Hmong, with better French language skills than Hmong language skills, may well find themselves communicating most effectively in Hmong, and in this way reversing the trend towards loss of linguistic and cultural identity. However, while these liaisons are a source of conversation and debate among the Hmong community, they take place very infrequently in comparison with the majority of marriages which take place among Hmong populations within nation-states, and therefore do not counteract the prevailing trend towards assimilation.

This trend towards assimilation correlates with disinterest towards the homelands in Asia, and even positive antipathy towards the idea of revisiting places which are felt to be backward and 'dirty'. Our fieldwork in Australia pointed clearly towards the conclusion that there was more interest in visiting Hmong communities in First World locations such as France and the United States, than in Thailand, Laos or China. There is still, among many of the younger generation, an interest in the Hmong identity and a sense of its importance, which is expressed in the fact that the overwhelming majority of marriages take place with other Hmong rather than with members of other cultural groups.

The need to find Hmong partners is a factor in the use of the internet by the younger Hmong community, and even by some of the old, but one is far more likely to find young Hmong in Cairns chatting with young Hmong in Sydney, Melbourne, or the United States, than with France or any Asian location, because of the fact that they can communicate in English.

Nostalgia remains important among many of the older generation, but this is more often appeased by watching Hmong videos or reminiscing about the past than in actual return visits or the use of the internet. Where return visits to Asian locations take place, these are most likely to be for a variety of practical reasons than for purely nostalgic motivations; among these motivations, by far the most common private motivation was the need to visit close relatives. But medical reasons also played a significant part in motivating these return visits.

Although further research is needed, at the moment it seems as though a significant transnational public Hmong community is emerging, albeit one badly fractured through political and religious schisms, among elite members of English-speaking nations; in particular Australia and the United States, and to some extent Canada. While nostalgia will probably always continue to draw some overseas Hmong back to revisit their ancestral homelands in Laos and even China, and nostalgia will continue to play an important part in overseas support for the Hmong within Laos, it is likely that domestic social, economic and political factors associated with particular nation-states will continue to play a determining role in facilitating or discouraging transnational Hmong flows and contacts of people, objects, signs and capital, as they also will in facilitating or discouraging Hmong assimilation and adoption into the countries of their new settlement. At the moment it is possible to find, as we found in Melbourne, a family with brothers settled in France, Australia and the United States, all in close contact with one another through a series of affinal connections, frequent visits, and the internet, and in close contact with other near relatives in Laos and Thailand. From such evidence it would be pleasing to imagine the future of the Hmong as a transnational community transcending the boundaries of traditional nation-states and forming a new kind of voluntary public diasporic community. However, our research shows that such cases are in the minority and do not appear to represent the dominant trends among the international Hmong community. While exciting and novel transnational contacts have been and are taking place, the practical constraints on these are too great for these to form a credible model of future trends.

While letters, cassette tapes, video tapes, and email are used to maintain transnational Hmong contacts and to initiate new ones, the majority of such contacts do take place between Hmong who are in different developed countries, such as the United States, Australia, and Canada. Similarly the greater majority of overseas visits seems to take place between Hmong in these countries. Thus the transnational Hmong community which is emerging through international travel and the use of modern means of communication is largely a community of the developed world, which to a great extent excludes Hmong from the developing countries.

While the global unity and reunion of the dispersed Hmong community remains an ideal and a hope for many Hmong, young and old, in the developed and developing worlds, the emergence of a global transnational Hmong community — a Communal Diasporic Voluntary Public Culture — is limited on the Web, as it is in real life, by a variety of social, political and economic factors. Many people in north Queensland and Melbourne told us they would like to go back to see Laos but had no money to go back, or had tried to but had had their visas refused. Moreover, the emergence of a global Hmong community of a unitary kind is prevented not only by practical constraints (mainly political or economic), but by the very real diversities of opinion within the Hmong community of a social nature, which make their presence felt on the Web as they do in real life. Thus there are differences between messianic and rationalist Hmong, those who believe in women's liberation and those who do not, those who support the resistance struggle in Laos and those who do not, Christian Hmong of various persuasions and those who follow traditional shamanic practices, besides the growing number of younger Hmong who have no interest in such issues.

What emerged very clearly from our research was the continuing importance of kinship in the lives of the overseas and Asian Hmong. Most visits took place to relatives, most new contacts were initiated by appeals to 'fictive' kinship, or the establishment of quasi-close kin relations based on clan surnames. The patrilineal descent system is often blamed, by Hmong themselves, for the divisions within the Hmong community which led to civil war in Laos, and there are isolated cases of attempts to overcome and reform it — by, for example, adopting a particular family name rather than a clan title as one of our informants in Melbourne had,[12] or in the attempts to establish new temples and centres and forms of worship which would unite Hmong from different clans, in Australia as in Thailand. Yet most young people even in Australia were still concerned to marry other Hmong, and to avoid breaking the incest taboo which operates between different clans. The extension of fictive kinship across the world, so that kin terms can be used between a Chinese and an Australian Hmong who had never met before, simply on account of their clan names, shows that from the point of view of kinship the Hmong already form a 'virtual community' (Pao 2002); the kinship system transcends the boundaries of place and can operate anywhere. The power of kinship was also shown in the many tragic tales of siblings, couples and children and parents divided from each other through the refugee exodus from Laos, and forces attention on the mechanisms these parted relatives have evolved for staying in touch. These include visits, economic cooperations, telephone calls and the internet. Yet real proximal kinship is inevitably damaged by long distance, and here it was often the case that actual kin relations were replaced by fictive or virtual ones.

If kinship, it might be argued, provides a *traditional means* whereby spatial distances can be overcome and vanquished, the internet provides a *new means* whereby separations can be overcome and new contacts established, and this inevitably plays a part in knitting together the transnational Hmong community as a community with an individual voice of its own. There is no doubt that such a transnational community is emerging. However, our research made the strong divisions of the Hmong community very clear, in particular between the newly educated, born overseas and largely English-speaking Hmong, and those who have remained in Asian locations. A further separation was observed between French-speaking overseas, and English-speaking overseas Hmong. It seems possible that in the future these divisions will become more apparent and more difficult to overcome, either through the traditional means of the kinship idiom or through the use of new technologies of transportation.

In broader theoretical terms, this project has shown the strength of the nation-state in curbing the emergence of transnational diasporic communities, and the power of local social, political and economic constraints in limiting the emergence of a genuinely powerful global public culture. It has also confirmed the association between overseas elite diasporic individuals and the support for conservative or insurrectionist movements of nationalism in their homelands which other research has pointed to. The importance of kinship in channelling, guiding and informing transnational relations has been demonstrated, as well as the continuing resilience of local places to redefine themselves in the context of broader global influences. The internet, as used by a minority of educated Hmong and particularly young people in developed countries, has been generally seen not as a vehicle for overcoming current practical or material constraints, so much as a means of communication and source of information closely reflecting the realities of social life. And while nostalgia is certainly a motivating factor in powering the returns to Asia there have been, it is by no means the only one and should be considered together with a variety of other practical reasons for revisits, in which the importance of the kinship system, as another space-challenging mechanism, stands out as primary.

Further research

At the conclusion of our fieldwork in Australia, although we have indicative and suggestive materials which we feel confident may be generalised to other locations in Australia and probably overseas to Hmong communities in developed countries like France, the United States or Canada, we became very aware of the need to undertake much grander surveys of the Hmong population, in regard, for example, to the direct relation between internet usage and overseas visits postulated in the original proposal (for which a default hypothesis was that the one might preclude the other), than the research techniques under this project have allowed. Indeed for the further development of a proper model combining local with global data, it may well be more appropriate to combine the traditional techniques of social anthropology (which can of course cover cultural and economic fields) with those of sociology and cultural studies. A combination of questionnaires with telephone interviewing would have allowed us to cover other Hmong populations in Brisbane and Hobart, for example, and to confirm or modify the conclusions arrived at from the data collected in Sydney, Cairns and Melbourne. Further similar surveys conducted in France or the United States would further have established how unique the Australian data is, or alternatively how representative it may be of other developed countries.

Footnotes

[1] Then known as the Colombo Plan for Cooperative Economic Development in East and Southeast Asia.

[2] Most lease on four-year leases from local landlords.

[3] With thanks to Maria Wronska-Friend for clarifying this for me, and for general comments on this chapter.

[4] Fieldwork was conducted also in Melbourne, and where appropriate I have included some of this data.

[5] This was formed after a conflict over the election of a Hmong Association president (later rescinded) whose wife was Laotian and who had close contacts with the Lao Association in Australia.

[6] I use the RPA transcription system, in which final consonants are not pronounced, but indicate tones, and doubled vowels indicate final nasalisation.

[7] Compare Wang (1998–99), who found households ranging from one to nine and an average of 6.1 members per household

[8] Some of those who were taken to the United States as children are now themselves adult; they have been included in the total population but not in the numbers of those who made overseas visits.

[9] 26 baht = 1 Australian Dollar.

[10] This case, which involved four business-related trips to the United States but none to Southeast Asia, is not included in those listed above.

[11] My great thanks to Yeu Lee, Canberra, for assistance on this project

[12] See Leepreecha (2001) on the effects of the adoption of Thai surnames by the Hmong in Thailand.

Globalised Threads

Costumes of the Hmong Community in North Queensland

Maria Wronska-Friend

There are very few societies in the world in which costume, whether an everyday dress or festive garment, has received such significant cultural recognition as in the case of the Hmong people. Costumes and silver jewellery have become for the Hmong their major form of artistic expression, a means of visual communication as well as a marker of ethnic identity. The Hmong costume adorns and protects, but it also sends subliminal messages about its owner's gender, group membership, locality, marital status, wealth, and so on. This study is based on research conducted during 1995–2003 among Hmong communities in Innisfail and Cairns in north Queensland, as well as in Yunnan Province, China, in June 2000.[1] The current situation of the Hmong costume in Australia will be analysed in terms of its manufacture, supply and use, as well as its function as a gift token, which connects the worldwide diaspora of Laotian Hmong migrants together.

Like all artefacts, Hmong costume should be perceived not only as a material construct but also as a manifestation of ideas and a means by which cultural categories and principles are encoded and expressed. Under the increasing impact of cultural globalisation, the analysis of Hmong costumes will assist us in understanding the social changes experienced by the Hmong at both a regional and a global level.

The Hmong Community in North Queensland

From the late 1970s to the early 1980s Australia accepted approximately 1,600 Laotian Hmong from refuge camps in Thailand. Initially, the major settlements of the Hmong population in Australia were in Tasmania, Sydney and Melbourne. From about 1996, north Queensland became the major centre of the Hmong population in the country, with more than 800 people representing 52 households and twelve clans in 2002.[2]

Cairns became home to approximately 300 Hmong people, largely Green Hmong (*Hmoob Ntsuab*),[3] while some 550 White Hmong (*Hmoob Dawb*) settled in the rural area of Innisfail, 100 kilometres to the south of Cairns. While the Hmong in Cairns earn a living by working usually as labourers in small industries and services, the Hmong in Innisfail work on banana plantations, which are usually run as family businesses. While many of the Hmong who live in Cairns have converted to Christianity, the majority of the Innisfail Hmong still follow their traditional system of belief, in which the shaman plays the important role of mediator, connecting the world of the living with the realm of spirits.

Migration and frequent changes in place of residence as a result of shifting cultivation have long been a well established tradition of the Hmong community. This aspect of the traditional Hmong lifestyle has continued to a certain extent even since their arrival in Australia. For a number of Hmong families, north Queensland is their second or even third place of residence in Australia, usually following initial settlement in Tasmania, Melbourne or Sydney. From about the year 2000, Brisbane started to gain significance as another place of Hmong residence, with several families moving there from north Queensland and other states.

It is most probable, however, that for a number of years north Queensland will remain the most favoured place for Hmong settlement in Australia. The local climate and vegetation are similar

Tossing the ball (*pov pob*) is a courtship game,
accompanying all New Year celebrations, Cairns.

to the environment they knew in Laos and allow similar food crops
to be grown for family consumption. At the same time,
involvement in farming in the area provides a number of practical
as well as cultural benefits.

The Hmong have a strong work ethic and it is important
for them to engage in meaningful, productive work, with all family
members being involved. Work on banana plantations, most of
which are owned by the Hmong, offers an opportunity of
employment for almost all family members, notwithstanding their
formal skills, qualifications or knowledge of English. In this
respect, work on banana plantations is similar to subsistence
farming in Laos, where every member of the family was involved
in some form of meaningful work according to his or her skills and
experience. The rate of unemployment among the north
Queensland Hmong is very low.

Another advantage of work on farms and plantations is a
much higher degree of cultural privacy than suburban life can
provide. It is much easier to conduct certain cultural practices,

especially healing or mortuary rituals which require the use of loud musical instruments or animal sacrifice, inside the sheds of remote banana plantations, than in the small suburban gardens of Melbourne or Sydney. Thus, the environment of north Queensland provides a significant degree of cultural autonomy that is vital for the community's well-being and allows a slow and controlled process of adjustment to the mainstream life of Australian society.

In the Village and in the Refugee Camps: Hmong Costumes Prior to Arrival in Australia

Evidence provided by older community members who had been brought up in villages in Laos during the 1950s and 1960s shows that in most cases the Hmong were traditionally self-sufficient in the production of everyday clothes. Hemp (*maj*), an important fibre of utilitarian as well as ritual significance, was commonly cultivated and processed. Natural indigo was the most frequently used dye, although there was increasing access to synthetic dyes. From about five years of age, all the girls were trained to make several types of elaborate embroidery and sewn garments — a skill which was seen as an important aspect of their female identity. Costume was an important marker of the group's image, and a code of dress which differed between each Hmong sub-group was strictly adhered to. It may have been these different types of costumes which resulted in distinctive names being given to the sub-groups of Hmong (Adams 1974, Bernatzik 1947).

In towns the situation was more relaxed, with many Hmong women wearing Lao sarongs, while the men often wore Western garments.

This situation drastically changed following the escape from Laos, in the aftermath of the Indochinese conflict of the 1970s, of thousands of Hmong who found temporary protection in the refugee camps of Thailand. Almost all the Hmong who fled from Laos spent several years in such refugee camps before emigrating to the West, and this powerful experience of displacement and social disruption had a major impact on their costume and textile art.

Hmoob Quas Npab — 'Striped' Hmong girl in a festive
costume, the components of which originated in four
countries (USA, China, Thailand and Australia), Innisfail.

After 1975, following the major exodus of the Hmong from
Laos, a chain of refugee camps was established along the Thai
border. Some of them, such as Ban Vinai, which at times had to
accommodate up to 50,000 refugees, became the largest gatherings
of Hmong people in the world (Conquergood 1992).

Many older members of the Hmong community in north
Queensland remembered that the escape from Laos had been a
watershed in the processes of change in wearing everyday Hmong
dress. As is shown in oral histories and photographs, traditional
everyday Hmong costume was replaced either by Western dress or
(for women) by a Thai sarong in the majority of refugee camps.
Hmong dress, however, continued to be worn on special occasions
such as the New Year, marriage ceremonies or funerals. In
photographs representing the marriages which took place in
refugee camps, usually both the bride and the groom wear
traditional Hmong costumes.[4]

The refugees were able to bring only a limited amount of
their personal possessions to Thailand, including costumes and
jewellery. The dramatic escape from Laos, which involved walking
for a number of days through the jungle and then secretly crossing
the Mekong River by raft and boat, meant that the Hmong could
carry little with them. Most of their treasured costumes and
jewellery had to be abandoned or left in secret places in Laos. In
some cases, silver jewellery was given to Lao fishermen as payment
for the life-saving boat ride across the Mekong River. In other cases,
Thai border guards confiscated objects of monetary value, such as
jewellery (Mr Ly Lao, Innisfail, personal communication, 1995).

Despite these circumstances, some Hmong managed to bring
small bundles of costumes which had special meanings for them into
the refugee camps. For instance, Sai Xiong carried with him a jacket
which he had embroidered himself — a very unusual task for a
Hmong man (Mr Sai Xiong, Innisfail, personal communication,
2002). Jou Yang, on leaving her home, took with her a jacket and an
apron which had been embroidered by her deceased mother. It
accompanied her to Ban Vinai and was later taken to Australia.[5]

Only a few such Hmong costumes made in Laos survived
the refugee camps of Thailand and were brought to Australia.

Hmong girls during New Year celebrations. The pink
costume was imported fom China; the other costume
represents new, composite type of Hmong costume, Cairns.

Those that did became highly treasured mementoes of life in Laos,
attaining the status of heritage objects, too precious to be worn. In
some refugee camps, there were instances of limited trade in
traditional costume with Hmong living in Thailand. For instance,
Jou Yang, on her marriage in 1981 in Ban Vinai refugee camp,
received from her aunt a white pleated skirt made of eight metres
of hemp fabric. The skirt was made by the White Hmong who live
in Thailand. Jou has never worn this skirt and never will — she
keeps it as a treasure, as 'a very special Hmong thing'. On the day
of her funeral the skirt will be deposited in her coffin (Mrs Jou
Yang, Innisfail, personal communication, 2002).

Silver jewellery, which in Laos and other Southeast Asian
countries was used by the Hmong as a store of wealth, was replaced

in the refugee camps by items of identical form but made of aluminium. These were frequently made from recycled tins in which food rations had been served (Mr Ly Lao, Innisfail, personal communication, 1995).

The abundance of time and the necessity to generate income in the refugee camps resulted in the creation of a new genre of commercialised textile art destined for the outside market. Under the guidance of craft advisers, new textile forms were created and produced in thousands of copies. These included pillow covers, table runners, wall hangings and various types of small decorative fabrics. Some of these were decorated with traditional designs copied from older Hmong garments and executed in reverse appliqué or cross-stitch. However, as most of these textiles were destined for the Western market, in which the symbolic language of the traditional Hmong designs was unintelligible, the Hmong changed the decorative style of their textiles from abstract, geometrical designs into realistic narrative representations which could easily be understood by outsiders. Most remarkable of these were the large pictorial representations of everyday life scenes remembered from Hmong villages in Laos, illustrations of ancient legends and myths of creation or, probably best known, graphic scenes representing the cruelty and trauma experienced during the war in Laos or during the escape to Thailand (Bessac 1988, Cohen 1990, Conquergood 1992).

It is probable that the motivation for the execution of these monumental fabrics was not only the commercial need for income, but also that their creation became a form of catharsis, providing relief from memories of war atrocities experienced in Laos and a way to expose the cruelties they suffered to the outside world. Catering to the Hmong demand for textiles, shops were established on the outskirts of the camps which sold the fabrics and accessories required to create Hmong costumes. In several cases, families who were accepted for migration to Australia bought, prior to their departure, expensive fabrics such as black shiny synthetic cloth (an upmarket version of the humble black cotton used to make everyday Hmong dress) from which new costumes were made to celebrate their arrival in a new country. Doua Yang, on his arrival in Hobart in 1987, took a photograph to commemorate this important event in the life of his family: both he and his wife wear

New year celebrations in Innisfail. The components of the costume are gifts, sent by relatives in overseas countries.

new costumes, made of black synthetic cloth purchased especially for this occasion from a shop outside Ban Vinai camp (Mr Doua Yang, Innisfail, personal communication, 2002).

Textile Art on Arrival in Australia

After their arrival in Australia, from the late 1970s to the early 1980s, the textile traditions of the Hmong underwent still further transformations, which reflected the very new social situation in which the group now found itself.

The very successful commercial production of Hmong textiles, which had flourished in the refugee camps in Thailand, has almost disappeared in Australia. Faced with new responsibilities and commitments, Hmong women, especially those employed in the horticultural industry, who had to look after their extended families, found that the pressures and demands of everyday life left little time to engage in the production of these elaborate and frequently monumental embroideries. Another factor contributing to the decline of this activity was the lack of assistance from external agencies in the distribution and marketing of the clothes. Some of the older, unemployed, Hmong women said that they would have been prepared to make commercial embroidery for sale, but were unable to get any support for the regular distribution and retail marketing of their products. Although in the 1980s Hmong embroidered cloths were occasionally sold from market stalls in Hobart, Melbourne and Sydney, the profit generated in this way was an additional source of income, not the primary source it had been in the refugee camps. Most of the embroidered pieces sold in this way were brought from Thailand as part of the migrants' luggage, or sent to Australia by family members who still remained in the refugee camps. A proportion of the profits was returned to relatives in Thailand (Mr Ly Lao, Innisfail, personal communication, 1995).

The case of the large embroidery piece representing the atrocities of the war in Laos which Mrs Poyi Thao of Cairns started to produce in 1986 in Ban Vinai refugee camp illustrates the difficulties experienced in textile production in Australia. The cloth was only completed in Australia ten years after her arrival in

Hmong girl attending New Year celebrations
in Cairns, in costume imported from China.

the country, in order to be presented at the Hmong textile art exhibition 'Migrants from the Mountains' organised by James Cook University in Townsville (in spite of the organisers' suggestions, Poyi Thao did not wish to display an uncompleted fabric). The reason she gave for the delay in completing this embroidery was the unsettled and busy lifestyle of the new country which was, she said, not conducive to the undertaking of such monumental projects, requiring so much time and concentration.[6]

The custom of wearing everyday Hmong costume, then, had in most cases already ceased to exist prior to the arrival of the Hmong in Australia, and it has not been revived in this country. The only part of the traditional Hmong costume which is still used in Australia in everyday situations is the baby carrier. Its continued use is due, no doubt, to its practicality: it provides the mother with freedom of movement and the opportunity to perform other tasks, while knowing that the baby is safe. Baby carriers are frequently sent as gifts by mothers and mothers-in-law to their expecting daughters and daughters-in-law, especially when a first baby is due. Mai Yang, who lives in Innisfail, has received nine baby carriers as gifts from her mother, who lives in France: each of them signalled the birth of a new baby. While some of the baby carriers were fully executed by her mother, others were made by Hmong refugees in Thailand, sent to France where the mother provided the 'finishing touches', and then forwarded to Australia (Mrs Mai Young, Innisfail, personal communication, 2002). I expand on the significance of these kinds of composite productions below.

Although in Australia the everyday Hmong costume has generally lost its meaning as a visual marker of Hmong identity, there has been one exception to this rule. In 1999, four Hmong families moved away from the mainstream Hmong communities of Cairns and Innisfail and settled inland, on the highlands of the Atherton Tablelands. The group started to use the name 'Amu' and established a new religious identity. The Amu believe that they are connections to the mythical Hmong emperor and have developed a distinctive set of rules and traditions to support this claim, including construction of a monumental temple. As an identifying mark, the members of this group wear in everyday situations either a full set of Hmong costume or at least parts of it — such as jackets, skirts or caps decorated with traditional Hmong designs (Mr Ly Lao, personal communication, 2002–2003).

The reaction of the mainstream north Queensland Hmong community members towards the Amu costumes is negative. Wearing an ethnic costume as everyday dress and trying to differentiate themselves from mainstream Australian society is considered to be an extravagant and unnecessary practice. According to the common opinion, the use of the Hmong costume is well justified on celebratory, festive occasions — but not any longer in everyday situations, where it is important to comply with the image projected by the dominant group.

Textile Production in Australia: Lost Skills and Gained Experience

Only some out of the diverse range of textile decorative techniques used by the Hmong in Laos continue to be practiced in Australia, and in most cases this is to satisfy immediate personal and family needs. Neither weaving nor dyeing of textiles is continued in Australia. Unlike in the United States, none of the Hmong in Australia make the batik cloth (wax-resist technique) from which the Green Hmong women's skirts are made (John Michael Kohler Arts Centre 1986). As a consequence, all the indigo-dyed skirts worn by *Hmong Ntsuab* women in Australia have to be imported from overseas — usually from Laos, Thailand, China or the United States. In many cases, industrial printed cloths imitating batik designs have replaced the fine, hand-drawn wax ornamentation. There is a somewhat different situation as regards the white, pleated skirts which are a distinctive part of the White Hmong women's costume. In Australia there are two women who used to make these skirts: Chi Lee of Innisfail, and another Hmong woman who lives in Sydney. The former, being an invalid for part of her life, was unable to work on the family banana farm and therefore had the time to be involved in the production of such elaborate garments. She learned the skill as a young woman in

Laos, as in her village all garments were produced at home. In Australia, she has made skirts in the same way, although white cotton has now replaced the traditionally used undyed hemp: all the skirts are carefully pleated and hand-stitched from nine to twelve metres of white cotton cloth, purchased from shops in Cairns. During the 23 years of her life in Australia, Chi Lee has produced about 200 white skirts, which she sold or gave away to family members. Now she is in her 70s, and poor eyesight has prevented her from making any more skirts. There were attempts to find a group of younger Hmong women to whom she could pass on this skill, but nobody expressed very much interest (Mrs Chi Lee, Innisfail, personal communication, 2003).

As regards embroidery produced for family needs, cross-stitch and reverse appliqué still remain two of the most popular techniques, practiced by older and middle-aged women. Reverse appliqué, practiced exclusively by White Hmong women, and which requires a very high degree of skill and patience, has been transmitted to a very small group of women in the younger generation. It has been largely replaced by cross-stitch which, even in its finest form, is much faster and an easier needlework method than reverse appliqué. Therefore cross-stitch patterns, frequently covered with protective sheets of plastic, dominate the decoration of festive Hmong costumes in Australia. The excessive amount of time and prolonged concentration required when producing reverse appliqué have been given as the reasons for its demise and the increased popularity of cross-stitch embroidery.

In Laos, needlework used to be the domain of women and an important characteristic defining Hmong womanhood. During New Year celebrations, young women used to be judged on their needlework skills, as careful handiwork used to signal an industrious, hard-working wife to a future husband. However, in Australia, a different set of values is used in creating a positive image of the Hmong woman and a different set of criteria is used in selecting a future wife. In public situations, young Hmong women still like to wear bright, eye-catching attractive costumes — but only in exceptional situations are they the authors of their own decorations.

Hundreds of hours spent on the painstaking execution of elaborate designs have little or no relevance to the lifestyle of the younger generation of Hmong women in Australia. Therefore it is quite difficult to motivate young women to learn these skills. In 2002, the Hmong association in Cairns, known as the Federation of Hmong National Culture, received a grant of $2,700 from the Multicultural Affairs Department office in Queensland to teach young women traditional embroidery skills. Whether this project will have any long-lasting effects, however, remains to be seen.

Costumes of Many Lands:
Australian Hmong Festive Garments

In spite of the demise of traditional Hmong costume worn as an everyday garment, it continues to play a very important role in the social life of the community as a festive dress. It acts as an important marker of ethnic identity, worn only three or four times during the year, on occasions such as family and community celebrations, especially during the Hmong New Year festivals and at welcoming or farewell ceremonies when a group of Hmong relatives or friends moves to another place. Of especial importance continue to be the New Year celebrations, when every member of the family wears a new set of clothes, usually richly decorated with embroidered *paj ntauj* panels. This old tradition of wearing bright, new clothes for such occasions continues to be upheld in Australia. This is to ensure prosperity for the coming year, and bring wealth and success.

The Hmong wear their traditional costume not only at events celebrated within their own community, but also when they wish to express their ethnic identity in regard to the rest of Australian society — such as at local cultural festivals, Australia Day, or when invited to attend events staged by other north Queensland migrant groups, such as the Buddhist New Year celebrated by Lao and Thai people.

As I have already mentioned, local production of Hmong garments and embroidered cloths is limited. The majority of the costumes worn on these occasions, therefore, have either been received as gifts from relatives living abroad or assembled in Australia from decorative elements produced overseas. An analysis of the origins of the components of several contemporary Hmong costumes worn in Australia reveals an extensive network of international connections established between the Australian Hmong and the rest of the Hmong diaspora. In outline, there are three major sources providing a supply of Australian Hmong costumes and their accessories.

Costumes as Gifts Received from Relatives

These gifts usually originate from relatives — members of the post-war Hmong diaspora, who have been dispersed to several parts of the globe. North Queensland Hmong have particularly close ties with family members who have migrated to the United States, France and Canada. They frequently visit each other and to commemorate these event, gifts made of fabrics, embroidered costume panels (*paj ntauj*), costume accessories (beads, silver coins), hats as well as full sets of garments are exchanged.

Light and portable, these costumes and their accessories function very well as tokens of memory and respect. Gift exchange of such items is a vital factor in building and strengthening the links between family members who settled in different parts of the world. In recent years, as a result of increased contacts with Laos, a growing number of costume components have originated from that country.

Commercial Products Manufactured in Thailand or Laos

The Hmong refugees from Laos who have remained in Thailand, estimated at approximately 10,000 people and concentrated largely around Tam Krabok temple in Saraburi province, have developed an impressive textile industry producing hand-embroidered accessories and full suits of Hmong festive costume. This production should be recognised as a continuation of the commercial tradition of the textile industry set up in the camps of Ban Vinai and Nam Yao during the 1970s and 1980s. However, the currently made textiles and costumes are destined almost exclusively for the Hmong migrant community, unlike the previous form of production which was targeted at Western markets.

Once again, the production of these textiles has proved to be an important source of income for the remaining Hmong refugees in Thailand, who receive very limited external support.

The most frequently produced articles are sets of finely embroidered matching panels which are stitched onto the apron and jacket (along the front opening, sleeves and collar). The blue-dyed pleated skirt, either decorated with batik or printed with designs imitating batik, is another popular article. Finally, a range of richly decorated hats are also produced for Hmong clients living overseas.

The commercial production of Hmong embroideries in Laos, although smaller in scale, is very similar to that in Thailand. These products are usually purchased during visits to Thailand and Laos and, on return to Australia, sold to local community members. Sometimes mail-order purchases are organised.

Industrial Hmong Costumes Produced in China

In the 1990s a significant textile industry was developed in the Wenshan area in the southern part of Yunnan Province in China, specialising in the commercial mass production of costumes for Hmong migrants who had settled outside Asia. Unlike the hand-made, commercialised embroideries produced in Thailand and Laos, these costumes are usually machine-made (including printed textiles and machine-made embroidery). Frequently the garments are made of synthetic fabric instead of cotton. The costumes are produced in bright colours ('shocking pink' being most frequently used) and decorated with strings of hanging beads. They are usually ordered from China and sold in Australia for $250 to $300 dollars each. This type of dress is particularly popular with young unmarried Hmong teenage girls.

In Australia, materials and parts of garments, many of which would be gifts sent by relatives, are freely combined with commercially produced or self-made costume components. An analysis of the origins of the basic components used in one costume, such as its fabrics, embroidered panels, beads, coins, hats or other accessories, can often identify several countries of ultimate origin, such as the United States, Canada, France, Laos or Thailand, reflecting the multitude of countries in which the members of one family may live.

In one such example, an analysis of the origins of the individual parts of a Green Hmong costume worn by Mai Yang of Innisfail during the 2002 New Year celebrations shows how widely some of the Hmong families have been dispersed, following their escape from Laos.

Mai Yang's family had been sent from the refugee camps of Thailand to three different countries: her three sisters had migrated to the United States, while her parents and four other siblings moved to France. She followed her husband to settle in Australia. The blue, indigo-dyed skirt of her New Year costume was a commercial product, made by Hmong refugees in Thailand. From there, it was sent to Mai Yang's mother in France, who enhanced it with additional embroidery and presented it to her daughter during her visit to Australia. The mother also made the hat as well as embroidering the panels of the jacket. The pink fabric of the sash had originated in Mexico, from where it was sent to Mai Yang's sister who lives in California, and then on to Australia. The panels of cross-stitch embroidery which decorated the sash were produced by Mai Yang herself in Innisfail, while the silver coins and beads had originated from Thailand.

The costume of her husband, Pa Chao Thao, revealed a similar diversity of provenance: the garment was sent to him from France in 2002, as a gift for the forthcoming New Year celebrations. His mother-in law (who lives in France) created an elaborate embroidery in the latest fashion of intersecting star figures. The fabric for this costume, a dense velvet, was of Mexican origin and had been sent to France by one of her daughters who had migrated to the United States. In this way, the fabric and the costume circulated half the globe — from Mexico to California, and then to France and to Innisfail in Australia, each time creating new meanings and establishing new links between subsequent groups of Hmong givers and receivers (Mrs Mai Yang and Mr Pa Chao Thao, Innisfail, personal communication, 2002).

A similar case of intricate global connections was revealed by parts of the festive costume worn by Sua Xiong. Although she had sewn the basic costume herself, some of its other parts and decorative elements were purchased or obtained from the United

States and Laos where most of her family lives. For example, the apron was a gift from her husband's relatives in California. One of the sashes was a gift from her sister who also lives in the United States, while she had purchased another one in Laos when revisiting her home area of Luang Prabang. The commercial fabric with floral designs which was used as a lining for the cuffs had been made in Japan, then exported to the United States, where her sister had purchased it, and subsequently sent to Australia (Mrs Sua Xiong, Innisfail, personal communication, 2002).

Today, it is quite rare to find festive Hmong costumes produced in only one country. In most cases, the contemporary costumes worn by the Hmong in Australia provide tangible evidence of the widespread network of kinship connections developed by the Hmong who settled in several parts of the world during the last decades of the twentieth century. Costumes and their accessories thus act as important agents in the process of binding the Hmong diaspora together and strengthening their international linkages.

New Costumes and New Meanings

Hmong costumes, even in villages in Laos, have never been an inert, static entity — quite the opposite, they always used to be dynamic constructs, ready to include new materials and designs, influenced by the vagaries of local fashion as well as encoding the collective vision of the community.

In the new social context of Australia, the cultural meaning and significance of the costumes have undergone major changes, reflecting shifts in the social identity of the group. The fact that contemporary Hmong costumes and their constituent parts originate from so many different countries of the world, illustrates the dynamics of these changes and has contributed to the creation of the frequently hybrid and heterogeneous forms of these garments. Both the form as well as the function of the Hmong costume in Australia have been significantly transformed.

Costume as an Expression of a General Hmong Identity

There is a growing tendency to use the costume as a means of expressing Hmong identity in general terms only, rather than identifying its owner as a member of one of the many Hmong sub-groups, as is still the case in the Asian homelands of the Hmong. For instance, in China, Thailand or Laos one can still identify a member of the Hmong community on the basis of the costume the person wears; the garment is not only an aesthetic creation and a testimony to the skills of its maker, but also serves as an external sign of a person's sub-group identity (Geddes 1976). In this way, it is easy to distinguish White Hmong from Green Hmong on the basis of the colour of women's skirts as well as the type of collar attached to their jackets, or the different cut of the trousers worn by men. In Australia, this very elaborate, complex language of visual communication has become greatly simplified, and with every passing year is understood by fewer people. The intricacies of the symbolic system of communication have become largely unintelligible to the younger generation of Hmong, those who experienced the devastating cultural shock of the refugee camps or who were brought up in Australia. The designs, the colours and the special cuts of the garments are rapidly losing their semiotic meanings. Thus, in Australia, the Hmong costume in many cases has ceased to indicate the sub-group identity of its wearer. As such, its informative function has been greatly diminished. The message it sends is one of being a member of the Hmong community in the most general terms.

As one of the Australian Hmong teenagers stated:

> I am a White Hmong, but apart from having a White Hmong costume, I also have a Green Hmong costume and a Chinese Hmong costume. In Australia, I can wear whatever I want (Melanie Lee, Innisfail, personal communication, 2001).

This statement is borne out to such an extent that in recent years several young Hmong women have started to wear Lao sarongs, made of lavish brocade fabrics, at the Hmong New Year celebrations. The preference for this type of costume has been influenced by idealised images of the Australian woman; the girls feel they look slimmer in sarongs than wearing the generously pleated Hmong skirts, while the brocade fabrics of the sarongs are shinier and look more lavish. After all, although it is not Hmong, this costume still originates from Laos.

Creation of a Composite Costume

In this situation, where the costume is in the process of losing much of its significance as a specific visual marker, the next stage is the deconstruction of the Hmong traditional costume and the creation of a new eclectic dress, composed of elements which traditionally were characteristic of several different Hmong costumes. This process of creating new composite costumes is especially common among the youngest generation of Hmong women, born and brought up in Australia, who in most cases are completely unaware of the complex visual language of the Hmong costumes worn in Laos. Varying components of several types of Hmong costumes are now grouped together in novel combinations. For instance, an indigo-dyed Green Hmong skirt may be combined with a White Hmong jacket and a round hat reminiscent of traditional turbans worn by the 'Striped' Hmong in Laos (*Hmoob Quas Npab*) and some groups of Chinese Hmong. The rules regarding the grouping of elements from various costumes into novel combinations are quite flexible. Strong visual impact of the dress, brightness of colour and richness of ornamentation seem to be the major criteria applied by the Hmong in creating their new ethnic apparel. Individual creativity expressed through this process is highly regarded. In many cases, one may observe a decisive shift from group expression towards individual creation in the forms of these new garments.

Hmong Chinese (Hmoob Suav) Costume

The third tendency characteristic of the transformation of Hmong costumes in Australia is the growing recognition of cultural connections with Hmong living in China, a country which is remembered as the original homeland of all the Hmong people. The relative affluence achieved by the Australian Hmong has allowed some members of the community to travel to China, visiting Hmong communities in Yunnan Province. This has resulted in establishing trade links and the importation of Chinese Hmong costumes into Australia.

These bright, mass-produced costumes, decorated with machine-produced embroidery, are increasingly used as everyday dress by young women from villages in Yunnan Province. In Australia, they have become popular as festive outfits for Hmong teenage girls. Every year, prior to the New Year celebrations, large numbers of these costumes are imported from China and frequently further embellished in Australia with additional beads, coins, lace, small bells and other decorative ornaments. In this way China, the Hmong's ancient homeland, has also been involved in the process of negotiating the new visual identity of the Australian Hmong.

The recognition of China as the ancestral home of the Hmong has further implications than the import of contemporary, mass-produced Hmong costumes. This is the place of the Hmongs' origins, with their ancient, mythical homeland believed to be situated somewhere on the northern plains of China, perhaps even in southern Siberia or on the steppes of Mongolia (Savina 1930). From there, several thousands of years ago, the Hmong believe that their ancestors started to migrate southwards. Re-establishing the connections with China through the importation of costumes creates an important new link with the country of their ancestors.[7]

There is no doubt that the contemporary costumes of Australian Hmong are extremely dynamic, continually changing creations, which provide tangible evidence of the group constructing a new identity and the growing significance of its international links. Although many of the Australian Hmong may not be consciously aware of this process, the costumes which they create and wear transform this non-verbal medium into a profound visual statement.

The Funeral Garment

In this very dynamic situation, there is just one type of Hmong garment in Australia which, so far, has resisted all major changes and retains its original form, as known in Laos. This is the funeral jacket, the powerful symbolism of which means that its materials and designs cannot be altered without negative repercussions on the whole community.

Therefore, although other Hmong costumes nowadays are made of synthetic fibres, the funeral robe and its embroidered squares of fabric are always made of organic materials such as cotton, which disintegrate faster, thus allowing the soul of the deceased a smooth passage to the other world. Metal parts, such as buttons, pins or metallic thread, are never included in the funeral robes, because the slow process of their disintegration would delay reincarnation (see also Tapp 1989).

Not only the materials, but also the designs of funeral clothes remain unchanged. The small geometric designs executed in patchwork and banding appliqué symbolise a person's possessions such as land, house and animals, and permit the deceased to take this wealth to the other world.

Many of the funeral jackets are sent to Australia by Hmong relatives living overseas — usually these are daughters and daughters-in-law who, in this way, wish to assure parents of their loyalty, care and respect. The funeral robes are given to the person during his or her life. By the age of 50, every member of the Hmong community usually has at least one set of funeral clothing, and quite commonly three or four.[8]

A very important part of the funeral costume is the shoes, which help the deceased to traverse the dangerous terrain on the return way to the village of ancestors. To ensure a safe passage, one has to wear a pair of special shoes, which are buried in the coffin. Traditionally, the shoes were made of hemp but nowadays the more easily available cotton fabric is used. In Australia there is only one person who makes 'death shoes' — an elderly Hmong man who lives in Sydney and cannot keep up with the demand.

In most cases therefore, the funeral shoes used by north Queensland Hmong are imported from Thailand or Laos (Mr Doua Yang, Innisfail, personal communication, 2002).

Conclusions

Although Hmong costume has almost entirely lost its practical function as a garment in Australia, it still continues to be an important expression of the group's changing identity. On festive occasions, the costumes remain the most visible manifestation of Hmong culture. This analysis of Hmong costumes also provides an interesting example of how aesthetics shift with new social positioning.

In Laos the process of costume-making and the associated transmission of skills used to bind generations of Hmong women together. In contemporary Australia, Hmong costumes still function in this way, but it is not the process of their manufacture but rather their circulation as gifts which binds and integrates Hmong family members together at a global level.

In a recent examination of theoretical models of cultural globalisation and forthcoming trends, Diana Crane has argued that in recent decades the concept of an homogenised global culture, corresponding to McLuhan's 'global village', has started to lose its significance, and is being replaced by a trend which recognises cultural globalisation as 'a complex and diverse phenomenon consisting of global cultures, originating from many different nations and regions' (Crane 2002: 1). In one such model, originally articulated by Appadurai (1990), cultural globalisation corresponds to a network with no clearly defined centre or periphery, where cultural influences move in many different directions and regional centres increase in importance as producers and markets. Although Crane bases her investigation mainly on an analysis of mass media, the examination of Australian Hmong costumes provides strong support for this model of globalisation, understood as a dynamic network of cultural flows.

The process of transformation of the traditional Hmong costume which I have presented here is based on research which was conducted only among one group of the Hmong diaspora — in Australia. It would be interesting to find out whether certain aspects of this process may be relevant to groups of Hmong migrants living in other parts of the world. I would expect that changes similar to the Australian ones may be occurring in smaller Hmong communities, in countries such as Canada or French Guyana. In countries with more numerous and cohesive groups of Hmong, such as the United States, it may be more important to maintain the proper form of the costume, in order to express the exact lineage and origins of a person. There is no doubt, however, that increased contacts between various groups of Hmong people living in several parts of the world will continue to stimulate the exchange of costumes and dress accessories as well as relevant materials and accompanying ideas. Will this process finally lead to the creation of just one, pan-Hmong costume worn by the whole Hmong diaspora? Or will it perhaps result in the development of distinctive national costumes, different for each country, so that we would be faced with a Canadian Hmong costume or an Australian Hmong costume? In another scenario, we may find perhaps hundreds of individual, diverse creations, inspired by what used to be the traditional Hmong costume of their homeland.

Today these questions cannot be answered, as it is difficult to predict the future course of social change and what impact it will have upon the transformation of the costumes. It is certain, however, that whatever form future Hmong costume may take, it will remain an important aspect of their cultural heritage, the visual symbol of their ethnic identity and pride.

Footnotes

[1] The author of this chapter would like to thank the following members of the north Queensland Hmong community for their ongoing assistance: Mr Doua Yang and Mrs Jou Yang, Mrs Poyi Thao, Mr Sai Xiong and Mrs Sua Xiong, Mr Ly Lao, Mr Sao Lee, Mr Pa Chao Thao and Mrs Mai Yang, Mrs Chi Lee, Melanie Lee, Mr Vang Yee Chang.
The fieldwork in Yunnan Province, China, was conducted in four Hmong/Miao villages, following the UNESCO-staged event 'Workshop on Transmission of the Traditional Technique of Costume-making of the Miao/Hmong people', Kunming, June 2000.

[2] Information provided by Hmong Queensland Association, Innisfail.

[3] The author prefers the term used by her informants, 'Blue Hmong', and this has been altered here by the editors, to accord with other chapters in this book. See 'Note on Orthography and Usage' in the introduction to this collection.

[4] For instance, the marriage of Mrs Sua Xiong and Mr Sai Xiong in 1979; and the marriage of Mrs Jou Yang and Mr Doua Yang in 1981 (Ban Vinai camp).

[5] Today in the collection of Queensland Museum, Brisbane.

[6] The cloth is in the collection of James Cook University in Townsville. During seven years spent in Ban Vinai refugee camp, Mrs Poyi Thao produced more than 100 embroidered cloths, which were sold through local handicraft shops (Mrs Poyi Thao, Cairns, personal communication, 1996).

[7] This reflects the views of contemporary informants, rather than actual historical fact. North Queensland Hmong, for example, refer always to a country situated in the north of China as their ancestral land. A good summary of various theories regarding the Hmong original homeland is provided by Schein (2000: 44–9).

[8] The severe, cold climate of the ancestral land requires that several sets of funeral garments will be placed in the coffin (Mr Ly Lao, Innisfail, personal communication, 1995).

The Private and Public Lives of the Hmong *Qeej* and Miao *Lusheng*

Catherine Falk

The Hmong *qeej*, sometimes called the *lusheng*[1] when used by the Miao in China, is a musical instrument which presents divergent and multiple personalities in its history, musical styles and contextual applications. On the one hand, the sound of this set of free reed pipes signifies death; on the other, it is used as a tool of public and happy display. In this chapter, I propose that the *qeej* occupies at least two spaces in Hmong thinking about themselves. The first space is for Hmong ears and eyes only. It occurs during funerals inside the house, the place of clan-specific behaviour and ancestral jurisdiction. It is private, proscribed, for Hmong audiences and communal Hmong benefit. The second space is overtly public and outdoors. There, performance practice norms are deregulated, and are intended as much for personal benefit as for communal well-being. At New Year and other renewal festivals, the *qeej* is presented as an icon of Hmongness for both Hmong and non-Hmong audiences.

An examination of the private and public lives of the *qeej* provides a refractory lens for viewing Hmong/Miao constructions of their identity, as well as their responses to changing circumstances. The manipulation of the *qeej* both by the Hmong and by the dominant societies with which they coexist exemplifies numerous ways in which the Hmong present their perceptions of themselves as a minority and marginalised group both to themselves and to others. These include firstly, the deeply held understanding that lost knowledge was regained and incorporated in the received texts communicated by the *qeej*, and that the essential meaning of knowledge regained is best preserved by being concealed and embedded within frames or layers of deceptive and outward 'noise'; and secondly, that ownership of knowledge and meaning can be controlled either as esoteric and internalised, or as exoteric and externalised assertions of identity (Cohen 1989: 69, Peterson 1988: 13).

Running parallel to these understandings are the theories that the body of meaningful knowledge about being Hmong becomes increasingly impoverished the further the population is removed from China; and that 'shared cultural space no longer depends upon shared geographic place' (Lipsitz 1994: 6). None of these ideas about Hmong 'self-conscious recognition of collective identity' (Peterson 1988: 13) is new, but when they are applied to the *qeej*'s performance contexts and musical structures, they furnish us with some interpretative clues about the contradictory nature of the instrument as a harbinger both of grief and love, as a vehicle both of intensely personal and symbolically communal communications, as an apparatus which both preserves the most serious archive of Hmong cosmology and presents a public face in which musical presence and meaning is primarily emblematic, and about the reasons why one of the most important Hmong texts is disguised so deeply that almost no one can understand it (Falk 2003b, forthcoming a and b).

In this chapter I attempt to reconstruct the private and public lives of the *qeej* through time and place, in China from the Zhou dynasty (about 1100–771 BC) to the present, and in the diaspora to Thailand and Laos and thence to Western countries, from the late eighteenth century to the present. The sources I have examined include accounts of Miao life by Han tourists in the eighteenth and nineteenth centuries, by Western missionaries, sojourners and ethnographers from the mid-nineteenth century, and by the Hmong themselves on the World Wide Web in the late twentieth century.[2] A cursory (and as yet undeveloped) glance at the *qeej*'s appearance as an accessory in Hmong stories[3] and textile arts adds a further ingredient to the tale of the *qeej*, and awaits a coherent interpretation. I will also demonstrate, briefly, how the musical structures used by *qeej* players differentiate its private and public musical repertoires. First, I will describe the many personalities of the instrument.

Qeej Roles

The *qeej* fulfils many roles in Hmong life, which I have broadly categorised as 'private' and 'public'. By 'private' I mean the restricted appearance of the *qeej* for a Hmong-specific audience, predominantly during funerals, where it is in turn a pedagogue, a speech surrogate, an entertainer and a psychopomp. At funerals, using *qeej* language, it instructs the soul of the deceased about death and the journey to the ancestral world. Inbetween its didactic duties, it entertains both the living participants and an invisible audience made up of the deceased, the spirits and the ancestors, all of whom are said to enjoy its music very much. Along with the souls of sacrificed roosters, it announces the arrival of the soul of the deceased at the doors of the kingdom of the Lord of the Other World, *Ntxwj Nyoog*, and at the realm of the ancestors. In its public manifestations, the *qeej* appears outdoors both for Hmong and non-Hmong audiences, where it is employed variously, as a 'girl-catcher' (a term used by Catlin 1997a: 79), as an emblem of pan-Hmongness, as a marketable and commodifed symbol of ethnic exoticism, and as an instrument of cultural revival and education among Hmong in the West.

I suggest that the *qeej* is used in its public role as a decoy, a 'double agent', diverting the gaze of others from its fundamentally secret life in funeral ritual. In a more political interpretation, the dichotomous representations of Miao by the Han as 'raw' (*sheng*) and 'cooked' (*shu*) can be applied to *qeej* roles. In its private role the *qeej* approximates the Han designation of *sheng* Miao, 'raw', or an unassimilated, rebellious and primitive people, while the public life of the *qeej* in contemporary China and the West embodies the virtues of *shu* Miao — 'cooked,' assimilated citizens of the dominant society.

Aspects of the *Qeej* Common to Both Roles

Some aspects of the *qeej* transcend the private/public dichotomy. Firstly, the instrument is played only by men, and I have suggested elsewhere that there are epistemological, as well as purely physical reasons for this (Falk 2003a). Secondly, organologically the Hmong *qeej* and Miao *lusheng* are differentiated from other multiple free-reed type instruments in China and Southeast Asia, such as the Han *sheng*, the Lao *khaen*, the Dong (Kam) *lusheng* and the Lisu *fòlú 'ò'ò*,[4] by their construction and by their position relative to the player's body. The Hmong *qeej* has a *wooden*, rather than a *gourd*, wind chest,[5] and its pipes run at right angles and horizontally, rather than parallel and perpendicularly, to the player's body.

Next, the *qeej* is a dancer, and its associations with dance date very far into the past. The movements of the dance differ in their form and intent according to the occasion. During funerals, the *qeej*'s prescribed and relatively sedate circling around the funeral drum transports the soul of the deceased and the message of the *qeej* from the world of the living to the spiritual world (Mareschal 1976: 261). However, at festivals and other outdoor occasions, particularly at times when young men and women get together, young *qeej*-playing men turn somersaults and otherwise perform spectacular feats of virtuosic acrobatics.[6]

The distinction between serious ritual movement and showy public dance while playing the *qeej* was confirmed by the testimony of two respected and well known *qeej* players in California, Nhia P. Xiong and Bla Seng Xiong.[7] They say that at funerals certain movements by the *qeej* player are required at certain times, including kneeling (*ntaus caug*) and walking under the hanging drum (*chaws qab nruas*), and these movements have special meanings. They must be performed correctly out of respect for the deceased and his or her family. On the other hand, they say, young players nowadays 'can put on a good show' (*dhia qeej*), but cannot really 'blow *qeej*' (*tshuab qeej*) — make sense other than making some sound. A true *tub dhia qeej* is one who can dance and still be able to play the words of the song correctly, and a real *qeej* master can tell the difference. However, this 'showing off' is also the proper way of presenting one's talents to the public (Nao Xiong, email, 18 February 2003).

The concept of the inseparability of choreographed movement and playing the *qeej* seems to be embedded linguistically. The expression *dhia tshov qeej*, 'to dance blowing the pipes' is discussed by Jarkey as a special case of 'co-temporal' serial verb construction in Hmong. In this type of construction, two actions are described by two verbs juxtaposed within the same clause, and can be thought of as constituting two facets of a single event:
Observe the following example:

Nws   <u>dhia</u>   <u>tshov</u>   qeej.
3SG   dance   blow   bamboo pipes.
'*He dances (while) playing the pipes.*'

Although these might seem like two distinct actions, in fact, to a Hmong person, they are inseparable: whenever the *qeej* is played, the performer's feet and body move and sway. Playing and dancing are not two events, but one. This assertion is supported by the fact that the verb <u>dhia</u> 'dance' can be used alone to describe the same situation:

Nws <u>dhia</u> qeej.
3SG dance bamboo pipes.
'*He dances the pipes.*' (Jarkey 1991: 169–70).[8]

References to the *qeej* in the travellers' and missionaries' writings frequently mention its role as a dancer (see, for example, Abadie 1924: 162, Agnew 1939: 17, Bridgman 1859: 286, Graham 1937: 31, Hosie 1897: 231, and Schotter 1909: 344). Lunet de la Lajonquière comments:

> Ils [Les "Meo"] dansent ... dans certaines cérémonies, les funérailles par example: le danseur ou les danseurs jouant du *sen* [qeej], le corps légérement penché en avant, tournent tantôt à droit, tantôt à gauche, sur un pied, puis

sur deux, sautent sur place, avancent ou reculent sans que
le haut du corps quitte sa position première et que le
chant de l'instrument soit arrêté (1906: 312).

A character in one of Graham's Ch'uan Miao stories tells
how

> When we study the *lusheng* we will secure good tunes.
> One who studies a tune should study a good way of
> dancing (1954: 102).

Fourthly, the *qeej* is most probably of great antiquity. We
know from myth, iconographic and literary evidence that the
multiple-piped free reed instrument type has existed in China for
thousands of years.[9] Although there is no proof of the longevity of
the instrument's use by the Hmong/Miao, Hmong stories about
the origin of the *qeej* attest to its function as a repository of
knowledge and its power to unite the voices of disparate people
(Falk 2003a), and place the invention of the instrument at the
beginning of Hmong history. In most of these Hmong origin tales,
the first *qeej* was made by men on the initiative of a divine source.
The Great Deity, Saub, or his support in some spiritual matters,
the Dragon, showed Hmong people how to conduct wedding and
funeral ceremonies using the *qeej* when knowledge, often in the
form of books and writing, was lost during the time of the Great
Flood.

Lastly, the *qeej* is animate, a living organism which speaks
and breathes. The names of its parts have anthropomorphic
attributions.[10] Xiong (1999) comments that the wind chest is
called 'the lungs' of the instrument. The action of the player's
breath and fingers on the 'mouth' (*ncauj* — mouthpiece), 'lungs'
(*taub* — windchamber) and 'fingers' (*ntiv* — pipes) brings the
instrument to life. Graham noted this: 'The *liu sheng* is alive, and
when played it is regarded as speaking' (1954: 9).[11]

The Private Life of the *Qeej*: Funerals

During funerals, the *qeej* addresses the soul of the deceased with
flowery poetic language for at least three days. Men first learn these

poetic texts of death as 'thought-songs' (Catlin 1997a, after Boilés 1967), which are then converted into *qeej* language using four of the *qeej*'s seven pitches to encode the eight linguistic tones in a process of speech surrogacy. Yang Lee described the process of encoding linguistic tone as musical pitch most eloquently when he said 'my fingers catch the words on my breath' (personal communication, Melbourne, 3 September 2000). The funeral speech of the *qeej* is not regarded as 'music': it is a set of instructions, a didactic liturgy (Pao Saykao, personal communication). The text transports the soul from the world of the living to the realm of the ancestors, binding past, present and future generations of Hmong clans. The correct performance of the *qeej*'s texts of death is essential to being Hmong and differentiates Hmong people from all others, as the *qeej*'s text demonstrates.[12]

The *qeej*'s instructions are only understood by the inhabitants of an invisible world — the soul of the deceased, the ancestors, and *Ntxwj Nyoog*. This audience hears and understands semantically meaningful sounds. To the living, the sound of the *qeej* is 'noise', although the combination of the sounds of the funeral drum and the *qeej* announces death. The meaning of the message is deliberately concealed so that living souls do not inadvertently follow the soul of the deceased on the journey of death. The *qeej*'s message is powerful and dangerous. It is disguised not only from the living, to preserve their lives, but also from outsiders or enemies, to preserve the integrity of Hmong identity. The contents of the funeral texts, both sung and played on the *qeej*, appear to have retained a remarkable stability over time and place (Falk 1996, and Falk forthcoming a). The Hmong funeral remains one of the most powerful affirmations of Hmongness wherever Hmong people are found, including in Western countries (see Falk 1994a, and 1994b). Funerals in the West are truncated facsimiles of those in Asia, for many reasons, but the presence of the *qeej* is mandatory.

Qeej 'music' at funerals buries and frames semantically meaningful tones in musical noise in both vertical and horizontal structures. The message is deliberately concealed in a complex 'web' (Catlin 1982: 193) of musical polyphony, drones, ambiguous communicatory 'noise' (Stern 1976: 129), movement, and poetic language. Semantic meaning is frequently framed within each song by lengthy sections of *qeej* 'noodling' (*ntiv*) in which the lower drone is heard, as well as the technique of 'sucking the *qeej*' (*nqus qeej*) to produce short detached sounds. Xiong refers to these complicated and difficult to learn passages as 'resting cushions', where the player can 'relax his lungs', and notes that they distinguish the beginnings and endings of songs (Xiong 1999: 3). Passages of meaningful pitch are embedded beneath the two upper drones and sometimes within clusters of other pitches. Communicatory 'noise' occurs in the frequent repetition of formulaic phrases, in particular the appellation *leej tub tuag*, 'beloved dead one', which when translated into *qeej* sounds is the iconic musical phrase of the entire funeral repertoire. 'Noise' is also inherent in the rules of *qeej* text delivery which demand, for example, that no two notes of the same pitch can be played consecutively, as this would obscure the semantic meaning of words which have different meaning but the same or similar spoken melodic and pitch contours. The noisy, loud sound of the second highest drone punctuates the delivery of both text and noise. It is produced by inhalation of breath. This blurted and insistent sound commands the dead soul to pay attention to the *qeej* (Yang Lee, personal communication, Melbourne, 3 September 2000), just as the frequently repeated identifying phrase *leej tub tuag* insists that the text is intended for the dead, not the living. The inhaled drone is used exclusively in funeral music; when the *qeej* plays instrumental versions of secular song (*kwv txhiaj*) the finger hole for this pitch is stopped (Mareschal 1976: 156). The upper drone sounds almost continuously. Music of death is characterised by the combined sounds of mouth organ and drum, semantically burdened pitches, the heraldic use of the upper drone, the repeated musical appellation which calls on the dead, and melodic phrases which are specific to each verse of the *qeej*'s funeral utterances. These characteristics distinguish the *qeej*'s 'death music' from its 'music for fun' (*qeej ua si*).

Knowledge of the *qeej*'s texts and true mastery of the instrument's funeral repertoire is an indication of great erudition and is accorded very great respect. Serious *qeej* musicians regard the 'showing off' by young players during New Year festivals as 'immature' (Xiong 1999: 2). Playing the *qeej* at funerals requires not only a prodigious memory, but also great stamina: 'One has mastered the *qeej* when he can blow flames of fire out of the bamboo pipes and unearth giant poles with the tips of the pipes' (Xiong 1999: 3). Knowledge of the *qeej*'s funeral repertoire does not come cheaply: the cost of lessons is two silver bars or balls, as Yang Lee told me (personal communication, 3 September 2000).[13]

In its private life the *qeej* thus embodies Hmong knowledge about Hmong identity in a highly respected and valued mode of social and musical competence. This knowledge is too dangerous to bandy about, and too powerful to reveal to outsiders or others.

Early Accounts of the *Qeej*

Early accounts of the use of the *qeej* in Hmong/Miao life in China, and later in Laos and Thailand, privilege its role in public festivals and courtship over its funerary duties. The earliest sources refer to the *lusheng*'s use among a sort of generic barbarian ethnic minority called 'Miao', and we cannot assume that they were Hmong. Later, we can partially track the use of the instrument among the White, Flowery and Black Miao in China, and among the White and Green Hmong in Laos, Thailand and the West. Nineteenth century and pre-World War II accounts of the use of the *qeej*, which specify ethnic provenance include, for the White Hmong, (or Ch'uan Miao or Pe Miao), Lunet de Lajonquière (1906: 311–12),[14] Schotter (1909: 344),[15] Seidenfaden (1923: 171),[16] Graham (1926: 305, and 1937: 31–2),[17] Agnew (1939: 13–17),[18] Lin (1940–41: 284, 330–1), Bourotte (1943: 38, 49 and 51) and Bernatzik (1970). The *qeej*'s presence among the Flowery (Hua) Miao is mentioned by Bridgman (from the Miao albums) (1859: 286), Clarke (1911: 63–6), Hudspeth (1937: 12–13) and Lin (1940–41). Mickey (1947) deals with the *lusheng* among the Cowrie Shell Miao.[19] Black (Heh) Miao and their bands of huge *lusheng* are described by Bridgman (1859: 286), Broumton (1881: 225–6), Hosie (1897: 231), Betts (1899–1900: 101–2), Clarke

(1904: 203–4 and 1911: 63–6) and Beauclair (1960: 144, 151–2, 170–1). Unspecified 'Miao' who use the *lusheng* are mentioned by du Halde (1736: 61–67),[20] Lockhart (1861: 185), Liu (1934: 31–2), Wu (1940: 842), and Eberhard (1970: 223–7).

Reconstructing the history of a musical instrument from an oral tradition based on written accounts by casual observers, whose agendas were far removed from contemporary musical ethnography, is at best serendipitous and at worst haphazard. There are, of course, no sound recordings from the distant or even quite recent past available for analysis or comparison. Nevertheless, some patterns emerge.

Pattern 1: Silence in the Early Literature about the Private Life of the Qeej

The nineteenth and early twentieth century reports sent home from Miao areas in China by European missionaries and officials are almost completely silent when it comes to observations of music in Miao life, let alone the *qeej*.[21] In musical matters, most evangelists were more concerned to teach the Miao to sing Christian hymns than to learn about indigenous music.[22]

The *qeej*'s private role in funerals is mentioned only among the White Hmong, starting with Schotter (1909), and Mickey (1947) for the Cowrie Shell Miao. All the other White Hmong sources listed above only describe the use of the *qeej* in public activities at festivals and in courtship. These accounts derive from travels in southwest China, with the exception of Seidenfaden, Lunet de Lajonquière and Bernatzik, all of whose encounters with Hmong took place in northern Thailand. Interestingly, these latter writers report that funerals are the *only* occasion on which the *qeej* is used: Bernatzik reports that the social use of the *qeej* is not customary among the Miao in Thailand (1970: 207)[23] and Seidenfaden is adamant that the *qeej* is only used at funerals among the White Meo of Chieng Mai (1923: 171). Detailed analysis of the musical role of the *qeej* in funerals did not occur until Mareschal (1976) and Schwörer-Kohl (1981, 1982) published the results of their extended ethnomusicological fieldwork among Green and White Hmong in Laos and Thailand respectively.

Even if they were invited, the earlier commentators probably would not have relished attending Miao funerals and spending three days and nights in the presence of a putrefying corpse[24] and in a constantly loud environment.[25] Silence or absence of comment about Hmong/Miao funerals and their music in these pre-twentieth century accounts does not mean that the *qeej* did not have a private life. As Brown pointed out in her (re)construction of seventeenth century Indian musical life, we need to read the ethnographic assumptions behind these travellers' reports,[26] and 'we have to be very careful not to read the frequency with which a musical subject was mentioned by European travellers as an indicator of its indigenous importance' (2000: 23).[27] Concepts about 'music', about its place in Western life as an elite art form, and self-consciousness about musical illiteracy or incompetence have contributed to a conspicuous aversion among many early ethnographers to engaging with indigenous musical production.

However, there might be more subtle reasons for this silence. Radano and Bohlman have argued that music possesses a powerful role in the construction of racial imaginaries. The alternative to listening to the music that is so inseparable from the racial imagination, they argue, is silence, but at the same time 'music has the power to undo the historical aporia of silence' (2000: 37). Further, they say, 'music gives voice to those silenced by racism … silence has also served as a racialist weapon because of the power accrued to it through the failure to listen to the music of powerless and voiceless peoples' (2000: 38). On the other hand, obfuscating *noise* aligns with silence as a mechanism for hiding meaningful sound. Perhaps the 'noise' in the literature about Hmong festivals, which seemed to become increasingly devoid of meaning for the Hmong and Miao, and the commensurate silence about their funerals, an occasion of the deepest ritual meaning and reinforcement of ethnic identity, was controlled by the Miao themselves.

Koltyk noted the silence in contemporary *pa ndau* (story cloths), in which certain Hmong activities such as opium production, for example, and funerals, are not usually represented, suggesting that because the embroidered cloths 'make a public statement about the Self for the Other, certain themes and subject matter are rarely reflected' (1993: 437). A form of essential Hmong knowledge, the funeral, is absent from, or similarly silent in the literature until serious ethnography of the Hmong emerged in the middle of the twentieth century. Bruner's (1986) discussion of the shift in the narrative structure of ethnographies about Native American cultures before and after World War II suggests that the emergence of a new narrative occurred when 'informants and fieldworkers come to share the same stories'. The Hmong after 1975 certainly had a story they were willing to share with fieldworkers as well as an army of sympathetic 'others', and studies of the Hmong incorporating Hmong voices proliferated after the flight to the West.

But let us return to the seventeenth century.

Pattern 2: The Public Life of the Qeej is Morally Questionable

The earliest reference I have found to the Miao *qeej* or *lusheng* dates from 1664. It occurs in an account of a moonlight courtship dance among an unidentified branch of Miao, provided by Lu Tze Yun in the *Pei Shu Hsü Yen*.[28] During the Moon Dance young men 'hold flutes which consists of six tubes, two feet in length. They probably have six different notes ... they blow and sing together' (cited in Lin 1940–41: 330–1). Lunar sports at which the *qeej* is played are also mentioned for the Flowery Miao in the eighteenth century Miao albums (Bridgman 1859: 260).[29] Liu mentions that du Halde, in 1736, referred to the use of the *qeej* for grand fetes and weddings (1934: 27). In particular, its role as a 'girl-catcher' is described many times. The *qeej* was an important component of a young man's courtship technique: nowadays, young *qeej* players are likened to rock stars (Catlin 1997b). Lu Tze Yun's description of the Moon Dance laments the morals of the Miao at these lunar sports:

> They blow and sing together with hands flying and feet dancing. Through exchanges of glances, motion of limbs and tossing of heads, their spirits are aroused ... To begin with immoral intercourse and after that to hold the marriage ceremony, this is the practice ... Oh! The Miao (cited in Lin 1940–41: 331–2).

Three hundred years later the missionary Hudspeth echoed this despair in his description of Flowery Miao behaviour on moonlit nights when the *qeej*, and others, come out to play. The *qeej* was, he says,

> ... the musical instrument par excellence ... played by the young men, who are popular and admired according to their ability to blow it ... [its tunes] play a dangerous part in the life of the young people. When on moonlight nights pipers come to the outskirts of a village the music is irresistible to the girls, who go out to the players, and after posture-like dancing and antiphonal singing spend the night in their company ... Human nature can sink very low (1937: 12).

The *qeej* as a 'girl-catcher' also appears in some of the Hmong stories in Johnson's collection. In one story, eligible young women admire a *qeej*-playing and dancing toad or orphan in the market place. Their parents say 'Girls, you should look for a husband like him' (1985: 231, 384). In another, the daughter of a toad wants to marry an orphan who played the *qeej* and danced while he played (1985: 161). The connection between toads, orphans and the *qeej* awaits further investigation.

The public life of the *qeej* is nowhere more evident than in the marketing of minority ethnic sound and colour by Chinese tourist agencies. Calendars of events advertise a variety of standardised entertainments including '*lusheng*' and '*lusheng* dance'. Miao, Dong and other minority villages and festivals are on the itinerary along with trekking, giant panda viewings, and scenic tours. The People's Daily Online (http://english.peopledaily.com.cn/200011/11 Accessed 20 August 2002), for example, advertised a 'Lusheng Festival' for November 2000 at which '1500 *lusheng* players' would perform; 200,000 tourists were expected. Wu Xiaoping points out that among this anticipated crowd would be Western Hmong 'seeking their origins' (2000). The *lusheng* shares the bill at ethnic festivals with bronze drum dances, costumed choral groups, lion dances, martial arts exhibitions, bullfights, boat races, archery, horse races, pole-climbing contests and athletic events.

Pattern 3: The Case of the Black Miao

The use of the *lusheng* by the Black (Heh) Miao came under the gaze of the missionaries Broumton in 1881,[30] Betts in 1899 and Clarke in 1904 and 1911,[31] and Her British Majesty's Consul, Alexander Hosie, whose 1897 account of the Black Miao (whom he calls Phö) is strongly reminiscent of Broumton's.[32] All four described festivals, but not funerals, providing quite detailed and very similar descriptions[33] of massed bands of enormous *lusheng*. Beauclair (1960) continued this tradition in her report of a visit to the Black Miao of southeast Guizhou in 1947. The Black Miao *lusheng* orchestras were spectacular.[34]

The Black Miao instrument differs from other forms of the Hmong *qeej* in its size, in its use in a musically organised ensemble, in the use of amplification devices attached to the end of the pipes, and in its position in relation to the player's body with pipes held vertically. Beauclair asserted that 'nothing like it can be found with any of the other tribes' (1960: 171).

Pattern 4: It Looks Like a Bird, Sounds Like a Bird, Dances like a Bird...

An association between bird imagery and the *qeej* instrumental type emerges from some of the earlier writings. Tradition holds that in the distant past the Han mouth organ, the *sheng*, was made to resemble the phoenix bird in shape and sound (Mingyue 1985: 36). There are iconographic as well as written instances of this correlation between birds and the mouth organ. I cannot offer a cogent interpretation based in Hmong cosmology or epistemology for this phenomenon. The association most likely starts with the images on the tympana of the fourth century BC Dong Son drums,[35] and continues in references in Hmong stories, representations in contemporary story cloths and written sources. In these sources, we find the instrument *sounding* like a bird, and its players *dressed* and *dancing* like birds.

Men playing mouth organs and wearing feathery headgear appear on the tympanum of the bronze Dong Son drums.

Representation of a mouth organ player with a feather crown on the Hoang Ha bronze drum (from Bernatzik 1970: 654).

Bernatzik described a scene on one drum, allegedly made by the Miao, as follows:

> In one of the houses one can see mouth organ players ... Beside each house there are two drums, each resting on a frame ... Between the houses armed men with large feather crowns on their heads are dancing ... A man with a crown, which presumably is made of argus-pheasant feathers, is blowing on a mouth organ (1970: 652–4).

The tympanum he is describing is that of the Hoang Ha drum. Mouth organ players as well as drummers also appear on the Ngoc Lu drum. The instrumentation suggests the Hmong funeral pair, the Lady Qeej and Mr Drum, but these Dong Son instruments have upright pipes, parallel to the player's body, not the right-angled pipes of the contemporary Hmong *qeej*. Catlin assumes that these Dong Son scenes depict the passage to the afterlife (1997a: 78), and Higham also suggests that scenes on the drums possibly show funeral rites, although they could also be fertility ceremonies; he notes further that these scenes are probably representations of aristocratic life, which certainly eliminates the Miao from the discussion (1996: 133). Imagery of birds (as well as toads and frogs) in general is prevalent in the designs of houses and boats on the drums, and in the feathered head-dresses of warriors and musicians. Bernatzik concludes, rather vaguely:

> The present absence of the feather crowns among the Meau is thus no proof that the feather crowns depicted on the drum were nevertheless not originally part of the cultural possessions of the Meau … almost all of the elements represented on the drum are not to be perceived as autochthonous cultural possessions of the Meau. *Only the mouth organ could be designated as a Meau element.* It, however, is much too widespread among other peoples to appear alone as valid proof [that the Miao made this drum] (Bernatzik 1970: 659–60, my italics).

There is no clear link here to the Hmong/Miao use of the instrument, although Bernatzik reports that a bronze drum from southeast Yunnan was in the possession of 'a Meau chief' (1970: 653). But possession of a bronze drum alone does not point to Miao possession of the mouth organs represented on the drums at the time of their making. However, Miao bronze drum dances are advertised by the Sichuan Provincial Tourism Administration along with '*lusheng* and bullfight', as attractions at the 'Miao's New Year' festival in its 2002–2003 calendar of 'traditional ethnic festivals in Guizhou'. According to Liang, the Miao Bronze Drum Dance was described in the *Book of Huangping Prefecture* and in the *Book of Bazhai County of Guizhou*; the bronze drum is beaten at festivals and weddings, and at new year festivals men play *lusheng* and beat bronze drums followed by gracefully dancing women (1987: 93).

The connection between birds, feathered headgear and the *qeej* continues to tantalise, however, when the befeathered mouth organ players on the Dong Son drums are compared to the embroidered images of *qeej* musicians which occasionally appear in contemporary Hmong textiles. In Figures 2 and 3, the position of the feet, the body posture, and the position of the hands are very similar to those of the player on the Dong Son drum in Figure 1. The players in these embroideries each has a small *bird* (rather than a feathered head-dress) perched on his head. The musicians' dress also shows animal designs, recalling Johnson's Hmong tale which describes a *qeej* player dressed 'in animal furs and feathery bird pelts ... all covered with animal tails and birds' wings and claws and beaks and eyes and teeth, furs and feathers' (Johnson, ed., 1985: 346–9).

Liang tells a story of the origin of the *qeej* in which its *sound* is likened to the singing of birds: 'the *lusheng* was made out of tree branches and bamboo to help in the hunt: the sounds it made imitated the singing of birds and the movement of animals' (1987: 82). The same source cites a passage in the *Book of Guizhou* in which 'some one thousand young Miao men and women dance like birds, playing bamboo *lusheng* and beating drums for three days and nights' (1987: 80). The Miao albums furnish us with more bird metaphors. Bridgman provides a description of an illustration of the Che Chai Miao ('Aborigines of the Chariot Stockade') in which three men play musical instruments each with a large feather plume in their head dress (1859: 260). At the Moon Dance described by Lu Tze-Yun in 1664, young men 'insert at the top of their hair chicken feathers which flutter gently before the wind. They hold flutes which consist of six tubes, two feet in length. They probably have six different notes' (cited in Lin 1940–41: 330).

Pattern 5: Loss of Meaning and the Impoverishment of Repertoire

The commentators report a progressive loss of meaning in the occasions on which the *qeej* appeared in its public life. In 1911, Clarke decided that Miao festivals had come adrift from their original religious purposes (1911: 63–4). Much later, Eberhard

Detail from 'The Flood': 'the orphan is dressed in a coat of animal pelts' (from Bessac 1988, frontispiece. Artist unknown).

'Orphan boy playing the keng'. Detail from the story 'Why farmers have to work so hard' (from Chan 1990: 14. 'Orphan boy playing the keng'. Artist unknown, cloth from Ban Vinai. Reproduced with kind permission of Anthony Chan).

reproduced Yü Chu-luan's *Reports about the Miaotse of Kueichou* (?1931) which noted that 'the real meaning of the festivals, which are undoubtedly a part of agricultural rites, has been almost completely forgotten' (1970: 223). The *qeej*'s use at weddings seems to have been lost long ago. Graham provides a story which tells how the Chinese stole the *lusheng* from the White Miao during a wedding (1954: 25),[36] and the wedding repertoire is now lost.

By the late twentieth century, Miao festivals presented for domestic and foreign tourists in contemporary China were almost completely devoid of meaning, according to Diamond:

> ...the only aspects of traditional religious activity that have survived are the socio-recreational segments of religious festivals ... which have been co-opted by the state as a purely cultural interethnic event under government sponsorship. The songs and dances have been revised to carry politically correct messages, the flirtations and pairings off that used to occur are discouraged. The audience ... is no longer limited to Hua Miao — it has become a cultural diversion for Han Chinese and others (Diamond 1993: 71).

The reification of ritual as performance events for tourists 'made the old people sad and nervous' (Wu 2000). Diamond notes that for the Flowery Miao the state-organised Flower Mountain Festival 'is a terrible time when crowds of drunken young Han men descend upon their community, trampling fields ... and making insulting remarks to young women' (1995: 112).[37] The degradation of traditional meaning continues when Miao performance arts are transported out of their rural settings to urban contexts. Liang proudly reported in 1987 that 'in the last three decades or so a number of excellent Miao dance programmes have been choreographed and staged in China. The dances were all developed from the Miao's traditional *lusheng* and drum dances' (1987: 93). Schein's analysis of state-sponsored and hybridised presentations of minority ethnic customs describes the 'dangerous crossroads', to steal Lipsitz's (1994) epithet, represented by these events at which there is a confluence of misrecognition of signals, firstly by the state as a rejection of feudal superstitions, and secondly by the performers as an enactment of nostalgia, all of it clothed in a false aesthetic (or anaesthetic?) of naturalness and authenticity. Schein cites the instance of *lusheng* players in Xijiang who refused to greet a delegation of Singaporean photographers, not wanting to play at other than conventional times, and provides the following theoretical framework which reinforces my argument that the *qeej* acts as a 'double agent' in contemporary Miao life:

> Codes of protected authenticity were being forged at the intersection of two complementary trends: an appropriative dominant practice that produced valorized tradition to exoticize it, and a proprietary subordinate ethos that recovered and conserved tradition to shield it from the corruption that dominant appropriation entailed (2000: 227–8).

Loss of *qeej* repertoire runs parallel to loss of ritual meaning. Tapp's 'theory of deteriorating knowledge' (1989: 114, 158) or 'epistemological entropy' (2001: 93) is illustrated by the loss of *qeej* repertoire. The diversity of vernacular *qeej* idioms seems to decrease as the population moves away from China. According to Mareschal, *qeej* genres for competitive jousting competitions and weddings were forgotten during the exodus from China, and an impoverishment of the repertoire of both music and dance is noticeable the further removed the Hmong are from China (1976: 198, 252). The *qeej*'s use as a speech surrogate implies that it spoke in regional vernaculars among Black, Flowery, White and other Hmong linguistic groups in China. The diversity of *qeej* dialects has probably been lost in migration; at least, the only detailed accounts we possess of *qeej* language are in Green and White Hmong from Laos, Thailand and Australia (see Falk forthcoming a).

Once the *qeej* reached the West, its appearance at multicultural festivals or public celebrations of Hmong New Year became almost purely emblematic. It is neither an income-earner for the Hmong nor is it attached to any deep religious meaning. Indeed, Scott described such events as 'mnemonic repositories' in which 'religious beliefs whose daily utility has ended but whose importance in maintaining a sense of ongoing ethnic identity is still very much in evidence' (Scott 1986: 245). The *qeej* has taken

on a globalised emblematic function as a symbol of pan-
Hmongness which is parallel to the iconicity of the didjeridu for
an essentialised indigenous people in Australia, propagated equally
by aboriginal and non-aboriginal peoples (see, for example,
Neuenfeldt 1997). 'Wherever in the world you are and you see the
qeej, you know it's Hmong', says Joe Bee Xiong of Wisconsin on
his web page (http://arts.state.wi.us/static/folkdir/xiong3.htm
Accessed 12 October 2003).

The *qeej* is now a tool for cultural revival in the diaspora. At
the Hmong Cultural Center in Minnesota, *qeej* lessons are offered
to young Hmong in order to 'bridge the cultural gap between
children and their parents, increase children's self-esteem through
instrumental lessons and build safe and healthy children'
(http://www.hmongcenter.org Accessed 12 October 2003). The
convention that restricted *qeej* playing to men has been broken in
the West. Weekly *qeej* lessons are offered to boys and girls in a
Long Beach Hmong Association initiative called '*Qeej* not
Gangs'.[38] Nao Xiong (1999), a high school student in the United
States, wrote about the *qeej* on his web-page school assignment in
order to 'learn about myself; knowledge of the *qeej* helped today's
generation to learn what it means to be Hmong'. Notation systems
for the *qeej* have emerged. Musical literacy certainly expedites
teaching to large groups, although the consequences of musical
literacy include a standardisation of oral repertoires, denying clan,
linguistic and regional specificity, and the loss of diversity in
interpretation and performance practice.

Conclusion

This chapter has discussed both how the Hmong perceive and
represent their most important musical instrument in its public and
private lives, and how Others represent the *qeej* by appropriating
the instrument, with Hmong complicity, for particular political and
economic agendas. Like its labyrinthine music, the *qeej* weaves and
is woven into a complex web of representations by Hmong for
Hmong and others, and by others for others and Hmong. The *qeej*
has trudged every step of the migratory trail with the Hmong, as

the story of of Chao Yang illustrates: he carried with him eight days worth of rice, an AK47 with 60 rounds of ammunition, and his *qeej*, sewn into a cloth bag, on his flight across the Mekong from Laos to Thailand; he and the *qeej* continued on to San Diego (Liu 2002). But in the West the *qeej* seems to occupy an essentialised position, announcing Hmongness both to Westernised Hmong and to Others through its mere presence as a remembered symbol rather than through its ability to impart deeply meaningful knowledge. The *qeej* is implicated in competing constructions of knowledge by and about the Hmong as they negotiate their new transnational networks around the world, with travel and telecommunication circuits linking members in real time, in virtual space (see Tapp 2001) and in remembered place. Ownership of the renovated Western *qeej* appears to belong more to Westernised Hmong than to *qeej* players who learned their art in Laos or Thailand. The public sounds of the *qeej* echo back and forth between the diasporic here and now, and a there and then remembered by Western Hmong but lived by mostly disempowered Asian Hmong. The contemporary Western *qeej* has added to its repertoire of roles, 'selectively preserving and recovering traditions, "customising" and "versioning" them in novel, hybrid and often antagonistic situations' (Clifford 1994: 317).

Examining the changing roles of a musical instrument is one way to test the coherence between sound structures and social structures which Feld suggested so strongly in the conclusion to his first and ground-breaking article about the music of the Kaluli:

> For any given society, everything that is socially salient will not necessarily be musically marked. But for all societies, everything that is musically salient will undoubtedly be socially marked (1984: 406).

The *qeej* has not yet been used in Hmong or Lao rock bands, as far as I know. Its private role as a conduit to the spiritual world has not yet been appropriated by the New Age movement, and its sound has not yet been sampled for exploitation by the transnational world music industry. But change is afoot: Roger Thao, an American Hmong, has devised an electronic amplification system for the *qeej* so that its individual pipes can be heard more readily at public events, creating an instrument reminiscent of the Black Miao *lusheng*.

In an optimistic version of the future for the *qeej*, it could be that the adoption of notation systems, the manipulation of the physical object as an artefact of identity-bestowing public display in multicultural environments, and the institution of group music lessons at which young people achieve a passing kinaesthetic familiarity with, but not mastery of the instrument, are examples of the appropriation, disarticulation and re-articulation of the communicative master codes of the dominant culture with Hmong-specific meaning, a process described by Mercer in the context of black independent cinema in Britain (1988: 59). A more pessimistic view would hold that the *qeej* will lose its private face as the exigencies of Western lifestyles and law cause traditional Hmong funerals to become increasingly difficult to manage, as knowledgeable *qeej* players die, as the conditions for the one-to-one transmission of an oral tradition no longer exist, and as the desire on the part of second and later generations of Western Hmong to receive this knowledge vanishes. The pre-eminence of showy dance in Western public *qeej* playing focuses the gaze on the individual performer, not the ear on the communal and community-ratifying message enclosed within the arcane and private texts. On the other hand, young American Hmong have learned of the significance of the *qeej* in Hmong culture by talking to their elders, and hold the instrument in high esteem, as Nao Xiong says:

> Knowledge of the *qeej* and its purposes will allow one to see more clearly what it means to be Hmong ... the *qeej* plays a very important role in Hmong culture ... It calms when one is frightened; it soothes when one is saddened; it leads the way when one is lost (1999: 3).

It remains to be seen whether the *qeej* will replicate in diaspora the diversity of its roles and vernacular idioms which it left behind in China, whether it will learn to speak with French, American and Australian accents in its private and public lives, or whether the assimilated, 'cooked' *qeej* will completely obliterate the quintessentially Hmong 'raw' *qeej*.

Footnotes

[1] *Lu sheng* means 'six pipes'. *Qeej* is the Hmong/Miao term; early observers sometimes picked this up in their transliteration. Clarke referred to it as the *ki* (1904: 203 and 1911: 64) possibly following Broumton's lead (1881: 225), Hudspeth transliterated the pronunciation as *ggeh* (1937: 12), Bourotte called it the *kreng* (1943), and Lunet de Lajonquière described a *sen* (1906: 311).

[2] Websites administered either by or for the Hmong include Hmongonline.com, Hmonguniverse.com, Hmongnet.com, Hmong ABC.com, hmongcenter.org and Click2Asia.com. Young Hmong also post their school assignments about Hmong culture on the web, many involving interviews with Hmong elders in the United States, for example, Ger Lor, Terry Liu, Lao Yang, Pheng Lor, and Nao Xiong.

[3] For example, Graham reports various stories in which a man is able to play several *lusheng* at once: in one, a man could play nine *lusheng* at one time (1954: 283); in another, a man could blow three *lushengs* with every step (1954: 23). Gold and silver *lusheng* make an appearance in other stories(1954: 235, 252 and 283). In some of the Hmong stories collected by Bessac (1988), Johnson (ed.) (1985) and Tapp (2001) the *qeej* is associated with orphans and toads.

[4] The pipes of the Lisu mouth organs are positioned away from the player's body, but its wind chest is a calabash (see Larsen 1984: 46–9).

[5] Moule (1908: 94) asserts that wood replaced gourd for the wind chest of the mouth organ during the Three Dynasties (220 AD–280 AD).

[6] Mareschal speculates that a *qeej* with short curved pipes is more manageable during the dances of the *qeej*, and this might explain the construction of the Green Hmong *qeej* (1976: 252).

[7] I am grateful to Nao Xiong who asked his father (Nhia P. Xiong) and cousin-grandfather (Bla Seng Xiong) about this matter on my behalf on 16 February 2003, and communicated the results of his discussion to me by email (18 February 2003).

[8] I thank Nerida Jarkey for pointing this out to me at the one day conference on Hmong research in Australia organised by Nicholas Tapp and Gary Lee during the Annual Conference of the Australian Anthropological Society, Australian National University, 4 October 2002.

[9] Pictographic inscriptions on animal bones and turtle shells excavated in Henan province and dated at least to the eleventh century BC are believed to depict the *sheng* (Yang Mu 1993: 21). Doktorski cites a Chinese myth in which the invention of the Han *sheng* is attributed to a mythical female sovereign in 3000BC (2000: 1). Its use in scenes of seduction as well as at ceremonies honouring the ancestors is documented in the Book of Odes (*Shi Jing*) (1027–77BC) and a *sheng* has been excavated from the tomb of the Marquis Yi, dating from 430BC. The *Shi Jing* (Book of Odes) mentions a 'reed organ' or 'organ' in six of its 311 poems, songs and hymns. The Odes of Wang contextualise the instrument in a love scene, where it is most certainly fulfilling its role as a 'girl-catcher':

My husband looks full of satisfaction.
In his left hand he holds his reed-organ,
And with his right he calls me to the room.
Oh the joy! (Poem number 67, page 50 of the electronic version,
1998).

Poem number 220, from The Decade of Sang Hu, finds the mouth organ
and drum performing 'to please the meritorious ancestors' as part of a
seasonal ceremony (page 187). Both public and private roles are reflected in
these poems.

[10] The reception of the sounds of the *qeej* by Europeans ranges from the cultural
relativists to the bewildered. In the first camp are the more ethnographically
astute commentators: for Schotter the *qeej* was 'doux et melodieux' (1909:
344); for Graham, 'beautiful music' (1937: 31). Among the latter, the sound
of the instrument was 'strange and booming' (Broumton 1881: 225); 'a rude
sort of music' (Lockhart 1861: 185); 'not unpleasant to the ear … but the
noise and confusion of sound has a decidedly depressing effect on one's nerves'
(Betts 1899/1900: 102); 'very creepy … and monotonous … certainly not
music, and soon becomes positively exasperating' (Clarke 1911: 64–5); 'weird
and monotonous' (Hudspeth 1937: 13), and 'very pleasant to the ear although
often a little too monotonous for strangers' (Wu 1940: 842).

[11] Because it speaks, the *qeej* is fundamentally a solo instrument: its message
cannot be heard if many *qeej* speak at once. Even when several *qeej* are played
simultaneously at funerals, they are not organised musically as an ensemble. I
speculate that during the *qeej* 'jousts' or *qeej* competitions, which Mareschal
reports are now defunct, the *qeej* engaged in antiphonal dialogue rather than
in a musically organised duet. The Hmong aesthetic for the sound of the *qeej*
demands that the individual pipes of one instrument should sound with
clarity — *phim* — when they are assembled, allowing the instrument to
speak clearly and sound good (*zoo mloog*). Each set of pipes is tuned to itself,
rather than to a theoretical norm (Mareschal 1976: 172).

[12] For example: You will see that the upper road on your right hand side is full
of the hoof prints of horses and cattle. This road is used by other people and
Chinese people for doing their business and trading. The road down there on
the left- hand side is also full of the tracks of horses and cattle. This road is
also used by other people and Chinese traders of fabric and thread. Oh dead
one, the road in the middle with clear still water which has no animal
footprints is the road for you to take to your grandparents' world. (Verse 11,
'The Song of Expiring Life', recorded on the *qeej* by Seng Thao, University of
Melbourne, 1992).
and from the *Qhuab Kev*:
… now you will come across three wells, don't drink from the upper well,
and don't drink from the lower well, these are for the Yi and the Han, but
drink only from the middle well … if you should hear another cock crowing
and your cock does not crow back, that is the path for the Yi and Han
people, but if you hear another cock crowing and your cock replies, then that

is the road of your ancestors … you will come upon three roads, one to each side, do not take the one to either side, one is for the Yi and one for the Han, but take the road in the middle, with dirty footprints and hoof marks, for that is your ancestors' road, that is the road for you (Tapp 2001: 185).

[13] Boua Xa Miao declared that 'when you play the *qeej* for a dead person it means you are giving him money. You know the saliva that comes out of the eyes of the *qeej*. The dead person's spirit looks at it as coins dropping from the sky' (Boua Xa Moua, in Faderman 1998: 35).

[14] Lunet de Lajonquière notes that the Miao play 'very agreeably' on the *sen*, a 'sort of organ' made of six or eight bamboo tubes whose sounds are produced by successively inhaling and exhaling (1906: 311–12).

[15] Schotter notes that the '*lou-sen*' , dancing and drumming occurs at funerals among the Pë Miao or White Hmong of southwest China: 'le son [of the lu sheng] est doux et melodieux … La rôle du jouer de lou-sen soufflant, sautant, se penchant tout le corps, incliné comme s'il allait s'asseoir, est fatiguant' (1909: 344).

[16] Seidenfaden translated a paper written by Luang Boriphandh Dhuraratsadorn, a District Officer in Chiang Mai, who described the construction of the *qeej*, and declared that 'music is only used on the occasion of funerals and not at other ceremonies. At funerals the Meo dance and sing' (1923: 171).

[17] Graham notes that 'in the hands of a skillful musician, [the *liushêng*] is beautiful music. Only men and boys play … and the player always accompanies the music with dancing' (1937: 31). He lists eight funeral contexts when the instrument is used (1937: 32). In an earlier publication he commented that 'the *luh sen* is not used at weddings, for its notes are considered too sad for such happy occasions' (1926: 305).

[18] Agnew, perhaps the earliest ethnomusicologist of the Hmong, devoted an entire article to the music of the Ch'uan Miao. He provides a lengthy description of the physical construction of the instrument and its tuning (1939: 15–17) and noted that, as well as its use with the drum at funerals, 'it is also played for amusement only by itinerant Ch'uan Miao *lusheng* players [who] may be seen in Chinese towns playing and dancing to ever interested audiences' (1939: 17). The full-blown use of the instrument as a source of income from outsiders is heralded here.

[19] Mickey wrote of the Cowrie Shell Miao of Guizhou: 'the *lusheng* is used by young men to entertain girls who dance at night' (1947: 49). The instrument was also used at bullfights, weddings and funerals (1947: 50).

[20] Du Halde describes life among the 'Miao tsee' of Sichuan, who are 'more cruel and savage than the Lolos, and greater enemies of the Chinese' and who play on an instrument 'composed of many small pipes inserted into a greater, which has a hole, or a sort of reed, whose sound is sweeter and more agreeable than the Chinese *chin* … they know how to keep time in dancing, and express in it, very well, the gay and the grave airs' (1736: 66).

[21] I have looked at 46 reports from China Inland Missionaries who worked among the Miao, dating from 1895 to 1948 and published in their journal, *China's Millions*. Not one comments on the use of the *lusheng*.

[22] For example, Heimbach wrote from his residency at the Shuicheng Miao church in Guizhou:

It was a real treat for me … to hear them sing such songs as 'I will sing of my redeemer', in good harmony … [after a baptismal service] the long file of folk wound their way back down the mountain, those baptized were lined up part way down and sang 'Christ the Lord is Risen Today'. It was really lovely and we knew that none but a risen Saviour could have produced such a transformation (*Field Bulletin of the China Inland Mission* 1948: 9–10).

[23] Bernatzik gives a detailed description of the construction of the instrument and the intervallic relationship between its pipes (1970: 199). He comments that the mouth organ (he does not give it a name) is 'a sacral instrument whose tone is pleasing to the spirits … [It is also] altogether pleasing even to European ears and resounds over many kilometres in the solitude of the mountains' (1970: 199). It is played only by men, and 'there are real masters but no professionals' (201); 'I never witnessed a dance where the mouth organ was not played' (206). It is used, in a 'cult dance', at funerals and burials (206–7). Bernatzik drew heavily on the writing of Lunet de Lajonquière (1904), who said that the instrument was used with dance when people were in a good mood, especially on market days when they imbibed heavily, or at New Year festivals conducted in order to please the ancestors; but Bernatzik says he never witnessed this, and concluded: 'Therefore I believe that a dance of the Meau on market days cannot be customary, since … dancing is connected with the use of the sacral musical instruments which of course are not used on market days' (207).

[24] Hmong in the United States told Symonds that *qeej* players 'absorbed much of the pollution as they breathed in the air while they played … proof of this, they said, was in the bad smell which these men produced when they passed gas' (1991: 252).

[25] Bourotte speculates that the sound of the *qeej* and drum was so loud that the deceased soul would be happy to depart for quieter pastures:

Le tam-tam bat, le kreng s'exaspère á la limite de sa sonorité comme si on voulait par cette débauche de mélodies saturer le mort de musique et lui faire concevoir les avantages du silence (1943: 54).

[26] See Alison Lewis's description of the encounters between CIM missionaries, Miao, Yi landlords and Han officials for an indication of the context of the reports about Miao life from the Bible Christians (2000).

[27] Alexander Hosie, of Her British Majesty's Consular Service, wrote about his travels in western China and was cogent and perspicacious in his list of reasons for the lack of depth in travellers' accounts of the minority groups. It is worth quoting his impressions of nineteenth century field work at length: Our knowledge of these races [Miao-tzu, Lolo,etc] is defective, for the simple reason that no foreigner has ever paid them a lengthened visit, which is

essential to a thorough grasp of their ethnological characteristics. Nor is this a matter for surprise, as the opportunities, which foreigners possess of visiting these tribes, whose haunts are removed from beaten tracks, are few and far between; and those few who have had such opportunities have been too much occupied with other work to study ethnological details or acquire a new language ... I passed through the countries of most of these tribes; but, like others, I found myself wanting in leisure to cultivate a closer intimacy with them ... In what does the traveller's day usually consist? He gets up at daybreak, hurries on to the end of the stage, writes up an account of the day's journey, endeavours to get something to eat, and tries to enjoy a few hours' sleep ere the labours of another day begin. The miseries of travel, too, breed a feeling of restlessness and a hankering after something more comfortable ... But all the comfort the traveller in these regions may expect ... is a shelter in a miserable mud hovel without chair or table — hardly a promising spot in which to commence ethnological studies.
Nor is this all ... the next difficulty is to find the man whose characteristics it is intended to study. The treatment which these aborigines receive at the hands of the Chinese, and the contempt in which they are held by them, have induced a timidity which is hard to overcome ... (1897: 225–6).

[28] Lu Tze Yun's description of the Moon Dance is much cited: see for example, Liu (1934: 32–4), Lin (1940-41: 330–2), and Eberhard (1970: 223).

[29] Bridgman, a missionary, gives translations of 82 sketches of the Miao-tze from one of the Han albums. Among the Che chai Miao, 'Aborigines of the Chariot Stockade', 'men play on instruments and women sing during dancing to the moon, an activity which leads to marriage' (1859: 260). Among the Hua Miao or 'Flowery Aborigines', 'young unmarried men play upon their reed organs' during 'lunar sports' in the first month of spring (276) and among the Heh Miao, 'Black Aborigines', there is a gathering during spring for a 'concert of instrumental music. The largest of [these bamboo] instruments are more than ten feet long and they are played by accomplished masters; others are very short and are used by the secondary players. To these they dance' (286). See Diamond (1995) and Hostetler (1995) for contextualisation and further discussion of the Miao albums, and Oakes for a history of Han colonisation of Miao 'borderlands' (1998: 94–7).

[30] Broumton, a China Inland Missionary, described instruments 18 feet in length, with mouthpieces five feet long and a foot in diameter. 'It requires a great effort to blow them and they produce a strange booming sound, which can be heard at a great distance. When playing ... the musicians moved slowly around the field ... there were five or six of these bands ... each with its circle of dancers' (1881: 225).

[31] Clarke observed thirty or forty groups each of ten instruments at Heh Miao festivals.

[32] Hosie's account is as follows:
The musical instruments are manufactured from bamboos of different sizes, some of them from twelve to fifteen feet long, fitted with a mouthpiece, their

lower ends being inserted in a large hollow cylinder (the hollowed out trunk of a tree) while the upper end of the longest reed is usually surmounted by a cone made of the sheath which grows at the joints of large bamboos. The instrument is called the *ki*, and from it a loud booming noise is, owing to the presence of a cylinder, extracted. The musicians move round in a circle as they play, followed on the outskirts by the young women (1897: 230–1).

[33] Brown has pointed out that travellers' narratives about India from the seventeenth century observed the convention of repeating observations of remarks made by earlier observers to verify the reliability of their own accounts (2000: 4) and I suspect that this convention applies to the descriptions of Black Miao *lusheng* bands — Hosie's, for example, is very similar to Broumton's (see endnotes 30 and 32); similarly, Bernatzik repeated much of Lunet de Lajonquière's work.

[34] Listen to Betts on the subject:

> ... there were thirty-six bands, six instruments to one band, and six sounds to one instrument. These instruments are named *luh seng* (six musical sounds) and constructed with bamboo pipes having brass reeds, emitting more noise than music. The largest- sized instrument is made of the trunk of a tree hollowed out, a bamboo pipe, 14 feet long ... Thousands of people have arrived from all the countryside ... The bands of six instruments form in line, standing shoulder to shoulder, in the circle formed by the spectators; presently six or seven damsels enter the circle and step in unison with the musicians, in a circular movement ... Heard from a distance the noise of these 36 bands (or 216 instruments), each playing its own tune, is not unpleasant to the ear, but in close proximity, where it is impossible to hear even one's own voice, the noise and confusion of sound has a decidedly depressing effect on one's nerves ... (1899–1900: 101–2).

Moule reproduces Betts' description of the Black Miao *lusheng* as the substance of his entry on the instrument in his compendious *List of the Musical and Other Sound-Producing Instruments of the Chinese* (1908).

[35] Some 138 of these drums have been found in Vietnam, Yunnan, Thailand, Cambodia, Malaysia and Indonesia since 1730. Depictions of mouth organ instruments occur frequently in their surface decoration, usually in the context of a row of dancers.

[36] Some considered the sounds of the *qeej* to be inappropriate: 'its notes are considered too sad for such happy occasions' (Graham 1926: 305). 'Grief and love are incompatible' (Xiong: 1999). Mareschal observed that 'the *qeej*, instrument of funerals above all, has no place in marriage rites' (1976: 198, translation by the author).

[37] See also Schein's description of Black Miao festivals as a form of 'internalising' and 'externalising' cultural revival in Guizhou (1989).

[38] The California Folk Arts Funding Program granted US $5000 in 2001 and 2002 to this program. At http://www.folkculture.otg/ctaap_grantees.htm Accessed 15 August 2002.

Being a Woman

The Social Construction of Menstruation Among Hmong Women in Australia

Pranee Liamputtong

Introduction

> Women, Women ... Well! if you don't have menses then you will not be able to have children, but if you have your menses then you will be able to have children (Fieldnotes 1994)

> Menstruation! People who are ignorant would say that it is a dirty thing, but it is the most important thing for you. If you don't have that you are not able to have children. If you don't have that you will not look healthy and it makes you look pale and unhealthy. If you have it you have no problems at all (Fieldnotes, 1997)

Menstruation is a universal physiological process in the lives of all women. But perceptions, meanings and practices related to it are not. As Buckley and Gottlieb (1988: 3) put it: 'While menstruation itself has at least a degree of biological regularity, its symbolic voicings and valences are strikingly variable, both cross-culturally and within single cultures.' Menstruation, as such, is viewed and treated differently in different cultures. In most cases menstruation is seen as related to procreation; it gives women power to conceive babies. But at the same time menstruation is seen as producing 'potentially polluting substances' (Delaney 1988: 80) and can cause harm to others, particularly men. Due to this, 'taboos' about it exist in many cultures. Very often these taboos are imposed on women's lives with the purpose of safeguarding others. These taboos have been interpreted as oppressive to women (Buckley and Gottlieb 1988: 6).

However, this does not mean that all societies see menstruation as polluted and dangerous to others. Hence, a universal assumption about the existence of menstrual 'taboos' may be problematic for some cultural groups. Buckley and Gottlieb (1988: 7) have argued this in their critical analysis of theories of menstrual symbolism. They point out that what is commonly found is a wide range of 'rules for conduct regarding menstruation that bespeak quite different, even opposite, purposes and meanings'. In this chapter I will demonstrate that so-called menstrual 'taboos' do not really exist in Hmong culture even though women may feel embarrassed about their menstruation. There are, however, 'rules' which restrict women's bodies and behaviours. These restrictions function to control women's bodies for another purpose; that is, for procreation, rather than protecting men from being harmed by women's blood.

In this chapter, the experience of Hmong women is used as a paradigmatic case to analyse cultural interpretations of menstruation.[1] I take Mary Douglas's (1966: 34) symbolic interpretation of purity perspective as a point of departure for my study, where she theorises that: 'all bodily emissions, even blood or pus from a wound, are sources of impurity'. Accordingly, menstrual blood, like certain other bodily substances, becomes polluting only when it departs from the bodily bounds of the natural order. As such, what is still bound within its body is not polluting.

The Hmong in Australia

The Hmong in Australia come from Laos where they lived as hilltribes in mountainous areas. Involved in the fighting between the American forces and the Pathet Lao (the communist faction in the Lao civil war) the Hmong were forced to move from their homeland in the mountains and escape to Thailand. The United States accepted the majority as migrants. There are over 180,000 Hmong people in America at present (see also Adler 1995, Liamputtong Rice 2000). In Australia, the number is far less than in the United States (under 2,000). The main concentration of the Hmong in Australia in the past has been in Victoria, though there are Hmong in Tasmania and New South Wales and now the greatest number is in north Queensland (see Lee, this volume). In Victoria, the Hmong live in close-knit groups, mainly in high-rise public housing in and around the state capital, Melbourne (Liamputtong Rice 2000).

Hmong beliefs are animistic and based on ancestor worship. They believe in reincarnation — the rebirth cycle. Hmong descent is patrilineal and patrilocal. Family names follow the clan system. There are ten clans in Melbourne. The average Hmong family is large. Most Hmong women in the study described here have approximately four to six children and it is likely they will continue to have more. Traditionally, the Hmong put a high value on having many children, particularly boys, since they could help in farming and continue traditional practices such as worshipping ancestral spirits, caring for their parents in old age, and carrying on the clan name. Such traditional customs are still practiced. In general, the Hmong are much poorer than other Southeast Asian refugees. The majority of Hmong people are unemployed, lack formal education and are still learning English.

The Study

This chapter is based on research in Australia among Hmong women who are refugees from Southeast Asia, who have migrated to Australia since 1975, but particularly in the last ten years. I conducted ethnographic interviews covering a number of issues concerning reproductive health, including the experience of childbirth, with 27 Hmong women in Melbourne. The demographic characteristics of Hmong women in this study are presented in Table 1.

The majority of the women had experienced childbirth while living in a refugee camp in Thailand as well as in hospitals in Melbourne. Older women were asked to participate so that I could learn more about Hmong cultural beliefs and practices. In addition, I interviewed several Hmong traditional healers (three shamans, two women herbalists and one magic healer) in order to obtain more in-depth details on traditional healing methods.

The women were initially recruited through a community centre they and their families frequently visited, and from the personal network of my bicultural research assistant who is a Hmong native-born woman. She has worked for and represented the Hmong community in Melbourne for more than ten years and she is well known and accepted by most Hmong in Melbourne. A 'snow ball' sampling technique was also used to recruit women into the study (Minichiello et al. 1995, Liamputtong Rice and Ezzy 1999; Ezzy 2002); that is, the women were asked to nominate or contact their friends or relatives who would be interested in participating in the study.

Entry into the community was sought from community leaders. I attended one of the community's fortnightly meetings and sought permission from the community leaders. Without their permission I would not have been able to conduct my fieldwork. The Hmong community was informed of my presence and the purpose of my research. In addition, I attended a Hmong women's Pap smear information day organised by a community health centre where a large number of Hmong attended. At the meeting I informed the women of my research and its purpose. I asked if the women would be willing to participate in the research project and if they could assist me. Most women agreed to help.

Women were contacted by telephone. Agreement to participate in the study was gained after information about the research and the nature of the woman's participation was clearly explained. Each woman was notified of the time needed for the interview. The date of the interview was then arranged to suit each participant. The women were individually interviewed in their own homes after informed consent was obtained. All interviews were conducted in the Hmong language by the author with the assistance of a bicultural research assistant.

Each interview was tape-recorded. The length of the interviews varied, depending on the women's responses. In general, each interview took between two and three hours. Most women were interviewed once. There were, however, a number of occasions when more information was needed, and those women were then visited for a second time, and in some cases a third time.

In addition, participant observation was used to observe and record Hmong cultural beliefs and practices and their experiences in Australia more fully. I attended a number of Hmong ceremonies and participated in Hmong activities. The main interviews and participant observation were conducted between May 1993 and July 1994. However, since the initial fieldwork I have revisited the community in order to obtain more up-to-date information and maintain contact with key informants, the most recent participant observation and several follow-up interviews were undertaken in 1999.

I situate my theoretical framework within the approach of phenomenology. The in-depth data concerning perceptions and experiences of menstruation was analysed using a thematic analysis methodology guided by phenomenology (Liamputtong Rice and Ezzy 1999, Ezzy 2002). Phenomenology, as Becker (1992: 7) argues, aims to interpret 'situations in the everyday world from the viewpoint of the experiencing person'. Phenomenology attempts to 'determine what an experience means for the persons who have had the experience and are able to provide a comprehensive description of it' (Moustakas 1994: 13). In this study, the interview transcripts were used to interpret how women described their meaning and experiences of menstruation in their everyday lives. Their responses were then organised into coherent themes (Liamputtong Rice and Ezzy 1999, Ezzy 2002), as presented in the following section. Verbatim quotations are used to illustrate responses on relevant themes. The women quoted are identified by pseudonyms.

Table 1: Characteristics of Hmong women interviewed

Characteristics		No.	Percentage
Age	20–30	9	33.3
	31–40	8	29.6
	41–50	4	14.8
	over 51	6	22.2
Religion	Animistic	27	100.0
Marital status	Married	21	77.7
	de facto	1	3.7
	Widowed	5	18.5
Level of education	None	18	66.6
	Primary	7	25.9
	Secondary	2	7.4
Current activities	Home duties	17	62.9
	Learning English for migrants	7	25.9
	Working	3	11.1
Number of children	1–3	7	25.9
	4–6	15	55.5
	7–9	1	3.7
	10 and over	4	14.8
No. of family	1–3	2	7.4
members living	4–6	11	40.7
in the house	7–9	10	37.0
	10 and over	4	14.8
Length of stay in	1–3	6	22.2
refugee camp in	4–6	3	11.1
Thailand (years)	7–9	6	22.2
	10 and over	12	44.4
No. of years in	1–3	6	22.2
Australia	4–6	13	48.1
	7 and over	8	29.6
Experience of	In Laos only	5	18.5
childbirth	In Thailand and Australia	15	55.5
	In Laos, Thailand and Australia	2	7.4
	In Australia only	5	18.5
English Proficiency	Poor	23	85.2
	Good	4	14.8

Menstruation: Being a Woman

The Hmong recognise that menstruation is an essential part of being a woman. Being a woman means to menstruate. The term commonly used by the Hmong to mean menstruation is *ua poj niam*, which literally means 'being a woman'.

> If you are a woman it must come. If you are a woman you must have menstruation. (Mai)

This 'woman-nature' is determined by a Hmong god who rules the Hmong world. A normal woman, therefore, must have menstruation.

> The 'period' is a natural thing for women. It is god-given and you will only have it if you are a woman. (Blia)

Menarche marks the beginning of womanhood among the Hmong. This is referred to as *nto nkauj nto niam*, meaning that women have finished their childhood and reached womanhood or motherhood. It is believed that when a young girl commences her menstruation she is capable of producing children. Dia explained:

> When the girl starts to have menses it means that she has reached motherhood ... Because when she has this she will be married and will be able to bear children. It means that you have the ability to conceive or bear children.

Menstruation and Health

At one level, menstruation is seen as 'bad' blood that must be expelled from the body. At another level, however, menstruation is believed to change the blood within the body. The circulation of 'bad' blood enables the renewal of the blood, which in turn will make a woman healthy.

> People say that if you have menses it is good because you have it every month and that is when it washes out the bad blood. (Joua)

The Hmong believe that women whose menstruation ceases for whatever reasons will be unhealthy. Women in this condition may become pale, skinny and eventually die.

> When you have your menses it is good. If you don't have it then you are like a person who is very unhealthy. Because you don't have your menses you are very pale and look like a person who is always sick. (Neng)

The clotting of menstrual blood is, however, seen as most dangerous to women's health.

> If you have clots and you don't have the menses anymore then you will die ... Like if your blood can't come out, it will clot inside your body and so you can't eat and become skinny and thus your blood inside your body will dry up and you will die. (Ntsi)

Dia told us about her relatives and acquaintances who had died from menstrual blood clotting.

> If you don't have the blood you will become skinny and then you will die ... There are three people that I know who have died from blood clots. They became extremely skinny and their face was not normal; it became very yellow. They had no strength at all and became smaller and smaller and then died. Our [relative]'s first wife died of blood clots. My brother's eldest daughter had that and died too. The [X] family's aunt died of that too. I saw them with my own eyes.

Menstruation, Pregnancy, and the Baby

Menstruation is seen as closely associated with procreation. For women, without menstruation, they are unable to produce children. Xao remarked that:

> For women it is a natural part of life and if you don't have it then you will be sick and look pale and just unhealthy. So you must look for medicines so that you can have it for good health and so that you can have children.

When asked about the relationships between menstruation and pregnancy, women offered two answers. First, menstruation 'makes the baby'. This is why women stop having menstruation when they become pregnant.

> People say that when you have no more menses it means that it has become the baby and that is why you don't have any menses ... Until you give birth to the baby and after one month you will see it again for one time, then no more. When the next baby is going to be conceived then you will see the menses again. (Dia)

Mai Koo used the metaphor of a protective dam to describe the relationship of menstruation to the baby.

> I think that when you are pregnant, it will stay inside and not come out at all ... I think that when you conceive a baby your blood and water will make a dam for the baby; like a dam would be for the fish. When the baby is born then it will come out with the baby.

Secondly, women said that menstruation disappears during pregnancy because menstrual blood is used to feed the baby inside the womb.

> Some women say that that is where the baby is going to grow from and that's why it stops and that menses becomes the baby's food. It may be like that because when you get pregnant you don't have that any more. (Mao)

Good Menses and Bad Menses: Health and Fertility

The Hmong distinguish between good menses and bad menses. The colour of the menstrual flow is used as an indicator of good or bad blood. It is believed that good menstrual blood must be bright red. If it is dark it means bad blood. Bright blood will make the woman healthy. By contrast, dark blood will make the woman pale and skinny; the indication of bad health.

If you have menses which is no good, like it is not bright,
then this means that there is a problem with your body
and that is why you are pale. (Mai Koo)

The flow of blood is also used to identify good or bad
menstruation. A moderate flow is believed to be best for any
woman. A combination of light flow and dark colour indicates bad
health. Mai Zong explained that:

For myself, if the blood comes a little bit at a time and
black then it is no good. If your blood is no good then it
will make you unhealthy. If that blood is very bright and
good then it finishes quicker and you don't feel tired, only
feel stronger.

The humoural quality of menstruation is also an
identification of good or bad menses and closely related to fertility.
This humoural quality is based on the hot/cold dichotomy, as
found also in the Chinese medical system. It is believed that 'cold'
menstruation contributes to infertility. Women were able to tell if
their menstruation was warm or cold, as Dia related:

You can feel it when you have your menses from your
body, if it feels cold, your menses is cold. Also when you
wash your clothing the blood will be black. That means it
is cold.

Good menstruation means good conception. Good
menstruation does not cause health problems such as back and
abdominal pains. Due to this, women who have good menses have
the tendency to conceive easily.

The old people say that you must have good menses and
then you do not have stomach or lower back pain for you
to be able to conceive. (Ntsi)

The colour, the flow and the humoural quality of
menstruation are also an indication of the capability to conceive.
When asked under what circumstances women may conceive, a
common answer given was as Nhia told us:

If your body is healthy and your menses flows properly,
then your menses is bright and that is how you can have

them [children]. But if your menses is not flowing properly then you will not be able to conceive.

Regularity of the 'period' is also believed to be an indication of good conception.

For good conception, the blood must be bright in colour. Also for those women who have irregular period they will have children very far apart; they will find it hard to conceive. (Nhia)

When women talk about infertility, very often they indicate menstrual colour and flow as its main cause, as Blia elaborated:

Periods vary from one person to person. It depends if they have always had only a little or a lot. If they have a little then they will have a little ... But [Y]'s wife told me that the reason why she can't conceive is because she has only a very small amount of period each time.

But menstruation with a heavy flow is believed to be the result of being 'hit' by spirits.

If you have too much menses then it is not good; small amount is better. A lot would mean that the spirit is trying to destroy your womb and that is why it has a lot of blood. (Dia)

Menstruation: An Embarrassing Matter

Despite the fact that menstruation is good for women's health and despite its importance for procreation, most women also see it as 'embarrassing'. This was reflected in interviews when I started to ask the women about menstruation. The following conversation illustrates this point.

Researcher: I would like to ask you about menstruation, is this okay?

Informant: What do you want to know about it?

Researcher: Well, anything that you can tell me, I think it is related to having a baby.

Informant: Is it? We are to talk about your body having
that dirty thing! Yes, you can, but what do you want to
talk ... With the Hmong, it is the most embarrassing
thing to talk about ... Yes, I am telling the truth, I became
a shameful person because of my menstruation; it flowed
too much. (Nhia)

When women no longer need to worry about the stain on
their *tia Hmong* (Hmong skirt) which causes such great
embarrassment, women feel somewhat relaxed about having no
more menses. Dia said:

With the menses, Hmong in the villages have no
underwear and no napkins so wherever they sat they will
leave a mark. This is very embarrassing. Whenever the
menses is due then you will worry a lot and feel scared
that it will show. So when you don't have any more
menses, you don't need to worry about it anymore.

The embarrassment was far greater for women in the past
when there was the fear other people might be able to see a stain
on their skirts or pants or even blood running down their legs.

I think that because it is unclean, it is unhygienic. In Laos
there are lots of people and if you can't keep it clean it
stains your clothes and you feel embarrassed towards
other people like the men around you and your children
and family. You will feel that they can see you. (Xao)

It must be noted that in Laos, Hmong women did not have
access to sanitary pads like in Australia. Women did not have
much to prevent the running of menstrual blood. In addition, the
scarcity of materials sometimes prevented women using anything
to wipe their blood away. If any sign of their menstruation was
shown, women were criticised for not being able to hide their
'embarrassing' parts, even by other women. Dia remarked:

What can you do! If someone sees it and if these people
like criticising others then they will say 'look at her she is
having that thing'. So this will make you even more
embarrassed. But some women will reply 'it is god-given

to every woman, don't you say that to me. Sooner or later
you will have that too'.

Men, particularly young men, would also talk about it if
they saw women with any menstrual marks on their clothes.
However, women also mentioned that despite this criticism, men
would not choose any woman who was not menstruating for
marriage, since they knew that such women would have difficulty
in conceiving.

> Men! If they see women having that, some younger ones
> will talk about it. But, like I said before, if you don't have
> it then no one will want to marry you. (Dia)

> When you are menstruating the men will avoid you and
> they will also talk ... I think they think that it is dirty.
> (Xao)

Due to this embarrassment, all Hmong women who have
reached menopause say that they feel much relieved. They also
believe that the cessation of menstruation makes them become
'clean like men'.

> When you are old and you don't have any more
> menstruation it is a good thing ... You will be just like a
> man. (Ntsi)

Blia, an older woman, told us about her embarrassment and
bad experiences with her menstruation. She said that she sought
herbal medicines to terminate her menstruation, which she
succeeded in doing. And so now she is 'clean like the men'.

> For me, I had bad menses and I hated it so much that is
> why I resorted to looking for medicines to get rid of it.
> I took medicines and so I am very clean like the men now
> ... I hated it so much that when it was gone I felt great.
> I was happy that I didn't have that anymore. I don't have
> to be embarrassed in front of other people any more. (Blia)

Those who have not reached the menopause have
ambivalent feelings about menstruation. On the one hand, it is
seen as essential for procreation. On the other hand, having it

causes uncomfortable feelings. Worst of all, if it does not come it
may mean death. Ntsi elaborated:

> Being a woman, that is very dirty and if you don't have it
> then you may be afraid of dying and if you do have it, it is
> an uncomfortable thing to have ... The elderly say that if
> it just stops by itself then it may be a clot inside your body
> and that is why it can't flow and this can kill you ... So it
> is unclean but if you don't have it you may die too, and
> also it means that you can't have children.

Dietary and Behavioural Restrictions

While menstruating, Hmong women do not have to take
precautions over their diet, except for foodstuffs which are
extremely cold, such as icy cold water and ice. Women believe that
drinking icy cold water will cause the blood to clot and this leads
to health problems.

> With food there is no restriction. Only that when you have
> the menses you should not drink very cold water because
> your blood will clot and that can make you sick. (Nhia)

> When you have menses you should not eat ice. If you eat it
> then your body will not be able to rid of the blood. When
> you eat the cold thing into your body it will make the
> blood clot and make you sick; pain in the stomach and
> you get all sort of sickness and this is no good for you. (Va)

Several women, despite this, mentioned that they could
drink cold water during menstruating. However, women who are
likely to experience abdominal pain while menstruating will
normally try to avoid it.

> Some people say that they if have no pain in the stomach
> or anywhere else they can drink it. For the ones that are at
> a higher risk of having stomach pain don't ... The ones
> that don't drink are the ones that have strong pain. Every
> time they have their menses they will lie down and at the

end of it they will be very skinny. These are the ones that will not drink cold water. (Xao)

The Hmong do not have many behavioural restrictions during the menstruating period. Women say they can perform their usual tasks and have contact with others in the community.

> When you have your menses you don't need to watch out for anything. You are allowed to do most things you want to ... For me I never stop doing any housework or other things. (Der)

However, there are restrictions which women are well aware of. These include not crossing over rivers, not washing their bodies or their menstrually marked clothes in rivers or dams, and not throwing the water used to wash off their menstrual blood into rivers. It is believed that these actions will offend nature spirits who will become angry and strike them. This in turn leads to miscarriage and infertility. Yee explained that:

> In Laos the old people would tell you that if when you have your menses and you go to wash your body in the river, the spirits there are able to trace you and hit you. If the spirits hit you and if you get pregnant, the spirits will damage it and it will come out [miscarry].

Mai, too, elaborated that:

> When you have your menses you should not go to wash these clothings in a river. When you have just grown up you do not know this so when you have your first menses your are very embarrassed about it so you go to wash your clothing in a river which is man-made and you must not throw the dirty water back into the river. If you wash your clothes and throw the water back into the river the spirit can 'hit' you and this will cause you to be sick. If you wash you must wash it and throw it into the soil. If you throw it into the river it will make you sick and when you get married it will cause you to not have any children and it is very hard to fix. You may conceive but it is only after a long time of healing that you can conceive.

While menstruating, Hmong women totally avoid sexual intercourse. Their main reason for this is that the men do not like it because it is dirty. For the women's part, they feel embarrassed about letting their husbands see their menstruation. They therefore try to stay away from their husbands and most men understand this behaviour and will not insist on sexual intercourse during this period.

> When you have menses you can't have sex with your husband because when it is like that it is very dirty … For us, we don't like it because when you have that [menses] you are very embarrassed so you don't even sleep near your man. (Mai)

Menstruation: Seeking Healing

> If there is pain associated with menstruation then you have to *ua neeb saib* to see what happens. And if the outcome of that is there is nothing wrong then you can just use the herbs to wash your body so the clots will dissolve and so you won't have any more pain … [But] if you are hit by spirits you have to *ua neeb kho* to separate the spirit. (Mai Koo)[2]

As this quotation shows, when women have difficulties with their menstruation, there are remedies Hmong women can seek to relieve their symptoms of ill health. There are two main healing methods most Hmong use.

Hmong Herbs

When a woman's menstruation does not flow properly or ceases, Hmong women resort to Hmong green herbs.

> When it does not flow properly then you use Hmong herbs to wash out the bad blood and the clotted blood. After this you will be back to normal … If the bad blood remains inside the body this will make you have stomach pain. (Va)

Women say that these medicines are wild plants. Some herbs are in root form but they may also be derived from the leaves or stems of a plant. Only those who are knowledgeable about this are able to gather them, and most of these people are old women.

Very often, however, women must ask a female herbal specialist to prepare herbs for them. The herbalist prepares a herbal concoction for them to drink, usually for three nights and once each night, and then their menstruation will flow properly.

If the menses does not flow properly then you have to go and *fiv* [ask] medicine from a *kws tshuaj* [herbalist] to give medicine for you to drink to regulate your body so that you will have the menses again. You will have to take it only two to three times before you will get better. (Nhia)

The herbal specialist must be asked for assistance and during this process, an agreed fee is negotiated. If the treatment is not successful, there is no fee to be paid. However, if the patient recovers, she must pay the agreed fee.

If your menses is clotted you have to *fiv* [ask] someone before they will give you any medicine. They will give you grown herbs and whatever they know they will use to help you. You will take the medicine and if it helps you then you will pay them the agreed amount. (Dia)

The fee charged by the herbalist is a sign of respect to those who have passed the knowledge to her. Without it, she will lose her healing ability. More importantly, if she persists in giving out such acquired knowledge without a fee, she may become ill herself and eventually die, or her herbs may become ineffective.

Txiv Neeb (The Shaman) and *Ua Neeb* (Shamanic Rituals)

If it is suspected that the menstrual pain of women is caused by being struck by spirits which are making them bleed heavily, a shaman must be asked to help.

If you know that this is what has happened [being struck
by spirits] then you must go to see the shaman and ask
him to fix you. It is only a *txiv neeb* who can help you.
(Neng)

To ask a shaman to assist in alleviating menstrual pain, a
woman must go to the shaman's house where his or her altar is
located, and formally request for help. Once this is done, the
shaman first holds a ritual to diagnose the cause of the woman's
abdominal pain (*ua neeb saib*). If it is diagnosed that she has been
'struck' by spirits, the shaman then holds another ritual to
negotiate with the spirits and perhaps bribe them to leave the
woman in peace (*ua neeb cais*). Traditionally, the spirits will be
offered a sacrificed pig and some 'silver-and-gold' money (in paper
form). If the spirits are malicious and do not wish to leave the
woman, the shaman will have to invoke his spirit assistants to
negotiate with them. Usually the evil spirits will be defeated and
eventually agree not to interfere with the woman's body. When her
menstrual pain ceases, the shaman must then perform the last
ritual, called *ua neeb kho* (the healing ritual). Traditionally, after the
healing ceremony, the shaman must be offered a sum of money, a
bunch of incense sticks, 'silver-and-gold' money and a live chicken
as a payment for his service.

Nevertheless, the Hmong may try both healing methods
when a woman does not recover easily. The following quotation
from Mai illustrates this succinctly.

My friend and I went to swim in a river and my friend
was menstruating. She washed her clothes there and since
then she was sick very often. Whenever she got her
menses she would be in bed for three to four days and she
was very pale. The family *ua neeb* for her a lot of times
and they looked for medicines for her too. After that she
was able to get a bit fatter [healthier]. Then we came here
[Australia] and now I don't know if she is able to have
children or not. She is still in Na Po Camp in Thailand.

Discussion and Conclusion

In many societies menstruation is perceived as 'pollution' because it is associated with dirt, mess and uncleanliness (Good 1980, Furth and Ch'en 1992, Rozario 1992, Prendergast 1994, Thuren 1994, Britton 1996). Good (1980: 149), for example, points out that in Iran 'menstrual blood (and the blood of childbirth) is not only physically polluting to the body, but is also ritually polluting. Menstrual blood is one of ten or 12 categories of *nejasat*, items which are ritually unclean, including faeces, urine, and the sweat of sexual exertion.' This uncleanliness of menstruation is similar to other forms of physical 'dirt' (like saliva or semen) which cross a bodily boundary. Hence, menstruation is symbolic 'matter out of place' (Douglas 1966). As such it becomes a 'pollutant' which is thought of as dangerous to social order. Due to this, rules or taboos commonly exist which are thought to protect human beings from the dangers of women's menstruation. Often menstruating women are 'excluded' from normal social activities such as cooking and looking for food. Britton (1996) and Buckley and Gottlieb (1988) point out that such seclusion of menstruating women has often been presented in negative terms; very often as oppressive to women. But feminist anthropologists have also pointed to the positive functions of women's seclusion or exclusion (see Rosaldo 1974, Patterson 1986, Gottlieb 1988, Martin 1992, Sobo 1992, for example). Rosaldo (1974: 38) argues that 'pollution beliefs can provide grounds for solidarity among women'. Women's seclusion in menstrual huts, for example, can provide a form of sanctuary for women. Patterson (1986: 490) contends that most of the women on Mogmog Island in the Pacific atoll of Ulithi in fact enjoy the break from their normal routines and 'spend the time happily talking or weaving'. Their place of seclusion, the 'women's house', serves as a community centre for them.

In many societies, too, menstruating women are not allowed to have contact with their men for fear of contaminating or killing them. Sobo (1992: 116), in her writing about menstruation in Jamaica, for example, points out that women who wish to secure the love and money of men will use their menstrual blood in cooking as a way to 'tie' the men to themselves. Here women's intention to 'tie' men to them is 'central to menstruating women's "unclean" state'.

But, as Buckley and Gottlieb (1988) argue, not all cultures have menstrual taboos and in some cultures there exists a belief in the positive powers of menstruation, besides its pollution (compare Douglas 1966). Kuper (1947: 107) pointed out a long time ago: 'in certain situations ... menstrual blood is not destructive, but is considered a life symbol or rather a life force'. In this chapter I have demonstrated that the notion of menstrual taboo does not really exist in Hmong culture. The Hmong belief that menstrual blood turns to nourish the foetus during pregnancy well illustrates this point. Similarly, in Sri Lanka, although there is a belief that menstrual blood is extremely polluted, the blood which goes to the baby is seen as beneficial (McGilvray 1982). The women in McGilvray's study believed that menstruation blood stops during pregnancy because the blood goes to nourish the baby. Good (1980: 150) points out a similar belief among women in Iran. Despite menstrual blood being seen as polluting, the potent quality of this blood is also seen as an essential element in reproduction. Women believe that menstrual blood turns into food for the baby during pregnancy. Delaney's (1988) study points to the same belief among Turkish women.

If we accept Douglas's (1966) symbolic interpretation as an explanation of this, we may see that menstrual blood, like certain other bodily substances, becomes polluting only when it leaves the natural bounds of the body. Hence, what is still bound within its body is not necessarily polluting, but potent. This interpretation is applicable to the Hmong women's explanation of menstrual blood as a substance which makes and feed the foetus during pregnancy. And this perhaps explains why menstruation, among Hmong women, is not seen as so 'polluting' as in many other cultures.

In Hmong culture there is no belief that menstrual blood may harm men, as there is in many other cultures, including the Thai and Lao. But nevertheless there are social restrictions which are imposed on menstruating women. Most of these are related to beliefs in the fertility of women; that is, they serve to ensure that women will be able to produce children. This can be seen from beliefs that a menstruating woman should not consume 'cold' food since it will make the blood congeal and causes ill health, and that menstruating women should not cross a river or wash their menstrual blood in a river, as the spirits may trace them through the smell of the blood and cause miscarriage and infertility. In this sense, as Gottlieb (1988: 74) argues, menstruation can be seen as 'a symbol of fertility, or life', not necessarily a polluting process.

In Hmong culture, menstruation is seen as an essential part of womanhood. This is due to its ability to enable procreation; as Gottlieb (1988: 64) puts it, menstruation 'embodies a symbolic principle that makes possible human fertility in the form of babies'. Procreation is believed to be an essential part of Hmong women's lives, which in turn is essential to the reproduction of Hmong society. But just why are procreation and the ability to produce children so important and valued? Taking a 'social structural perspective', Inhorn (1996) argues that children are important for three main reasons. First, children are necessary in order to ensure the survival of their parents and families. Second, in most patriarchal societies children are the only 'valuable power resource' for their mothers. Hence, having children can improve the status of women. Third, children are needed for the continuation of the society itself.

In Hmong culture, children are necessary for one's well-being, not only in this life but also in the afterlife. This ensures the continuation of the family, lineage and clan. Without children, neither Hmong men nor women are perceived as complete. While Hmong girls and women do not have equal social or familial status to Hmong boys and men, their status changes when they marry and are able to bear a child. The birth of the first child brings prestige to a Hmong woman. Women gain respect and status when they produce children (Liamputtong 2002; Liamputtong Rice 1995, 1998, 2000; Symonds 1991, 1996). All these cultural expectations make menstruation an essential part of women's lives.

In conclusion, this study has provided readers with a cultural perspective on menstruation practices and beliefs among Hmong women now living in Australia. As Layne (1990: 70) has argued, 'the anthropological approach, with its emphasis on the cultural construction of meanings and special understanding of ritual process' provides a crucial dimension for research into women and reproduction. If we are to truly understand the rich reality of women's lives, we must see menstruation within the context of culture. This is particularly so in Australian society where the cultural diversity of immigrant women is so great.

Acknowledgements

I am indebted to Hmong women for their time and knowledge given to me during my fieldwork and afterwards. I am grateful to Blia Ly, my bicultural research assistant who assisted me during the fieldwork and subsequently in the process of analysis.

Footnotes

[1] This chapter is a revised and edited version of the chapter on menstruation in Liamputtong Rice (2000).
[2] *Ua neeb saib* and *ua neeb kho* are two parts of the shamanic healing session. See below.

Process and Goal
in White Hmong

Nerida Jarkey

Introduction

My investigation of the White Hmong language was made possible
through the kindness and generosity of my primary language
teacher, Cua Lis, and her family: Cua's husband Choj (Sao), Choj's
brothers Yeeb, Nkaj Yias (Gary), and Ntxawg (Yeu), and their dear
mother Maiv Yaj. I also received enthusiastic help from Charlie
Sayaxang, Sourivan Thongpao, Maiv Dub Yaj, and Ge and Niaj
Pov Lis. Cua and her family originally came from Xieng Khoung
province in Laos and, at the time I conducted the basic research for
this investigation during the mid 1980s to early 1990s, they lived
in Sydney, Australia.

To all of these wonderful people, and especially to Cua,
I am grateful not only for help in learning about language but also
for help in learning about life. Quite early on in the course of my
research I gave birth to my first child, Alex. Cua already had her
first son, William, and had recently given birth to her second,
Matthew. Cua was like a big sister to me and I treasure, more than
I can say, her friendship and guidance in those early years of
motherhood. Not too far along the track, my second son, Dom,

and Cua's daughter, Melanie, arrived too. Perhaps it's not surprising that my memories of visiting Cua to learn Hmong are intricately tied with my memories of pregnancy, birth, exhaustion, joy, and lots and lots of noise!

As we sat feeding our babies together, a casual observer might have been struck by our differences: Cua short, dark-skinned, and glowing with good health and strength, and I, tall, fair-skinned and looking (and feeling) as if a slight breeze would blow me over. Yet one warm and reassuring thing that Cua often used to say as we sat down together to feed the babies still stands out in my memory: 'We're all the same'!

In some ways, that's just what this chapter is all about. In it I discuss an aspect of language — the expression of process and goal — in which Hmong and English appear to exhibit very different modes of expression. While these differences are extremely interesting and important to acknowledge, I conclude, however, that they should not be taken as indicative of any underlying differences in the way that speakers of these two languages fundamentally conceive of the notions described. They should simply be understood, instead, as attributable to the way that two typologically distinct languages distribute semantic information within the clause.

Summary of the Argument

This chapter investigates how processes that have goals are represented in the White Hmong language, and discusses the ways in which the representation of such processes in Hmong differs from that in English. The chapter deals with two kinds of processes: those that have intrinsic goals and those that have extrinsic goals.

Processes that have intrinsic goals, like xaws ib daig tiab 'sew a skirt', are *telic*: they are processes that come to an inevitable terminal point, after which they can no longer continue. In other words, if you keep on 'sewing a skirt', you will eventually 'have sewn the skirt'; you just can't keep on sewing the same skirt forever! This kind of process is quite different from a process that has an extrinsic goal, such as <u>nrhiav kuv nti nplhaib</u> 'search for my ring'. Processes like this are *atelic*: they have no inevitable terminal point. One might keep on 'searching for one's ring' forever, without ever finding it.

The primary difference between English and Hmong with respect to these goal-oriented processes is related to the way in which the attainment of the goal is expressed. In English, the attainment of goal of the two different kinds of goal-oriented processes — those with intrinsic goals and those with extrinsic goals — is expressed in two quite different ways. To express the attainment of an intrinsic goal one simply uses a different form of the same verb that is used to describe the goal-oriented process, while to express the attainment of an extrinsic goal one must use an entirely different verb.

In Hmong, however, the attainment of both an intrinsic and an extrinsic goal is expressed in basically the same way. When the focus is on the process itself, a simple verb is used. When the focus is on the attainment of the goal (whether intrinsic or extrinsic), a Serial Verb Construction is used. In these 'Attainment Serial Verb Constructions', two verbs appear in a single clause: the first describes the process and the second describes the attainment of the goal.

These differences in expression should not be thought of as suggesting any fundamental difference between the ways in which speakers of these two languages conceptualise the notion of attainment of goal. Instead, it should simply be seen as a result of the way in which these two typologically distinct languages deal with this particular language function.

A First Glance at the Differences: Hmong and English

There are a number of different kinds of actions involving processes that have goals. Observe the following examples in Hmong and their translations in English:

(1)   xaws   daig   tiab   no
      sew   CLF   skirt this
      '*sew this skirt*'

(2)   nrhiav kuv   nti   nplhaib
      search 1SG   CLF   ring
      '*search for my ring*'

Both of these examples describe an action that occurs over time (a process), and that has a clear purpose (a goal). One sews a skirt (Example (1)) in order to get a new skirt. One searches for a ring (Example (2)) in order to find the ring.

There are some interesting differences, however, in the ways in which the attainment of the goals of these two processes is expressed in Hmong and in English. These are shown in Examples (1') and (2').

(1') Nws   xaws   tau   daig   tiab   no.
      3SG   sew   get   CLF   skirt this
      '*She *sewed* this skirt.*'

(2') Kuv   nrhiav tau   kuv   nti   nplhaib.
      1SG   search get   1SG   CLF   ring
      '*I *found* my ring.*'

The Hmong sentences in (1') and (2') are similar to one another, and also similar to the Hmong examples (1) and (2) respectively. In each case, the attainment of the goal is expressed by simply adding the verb tau 'get' after the verb that indicates the goal-oriented process (xaws 'sew' in (1') and nrhiav 'search' in (2')). Looking only at the Hmong examples (1) and (1'), we might assume that tau is simply a marker of past tense: xaws 'sew', xaws tau 'sewed'. Examples (2) and (2') show us clearly that this is not the case. While nrhiav in (1) means 'search', nhriav tau in (1') means not 'searched' but 'found'. The verb tau 'get' appearing after the verbs xaws and nhriav in these sentences functions not to mark past tense, but to indicate that the goal is attained.[1] Sequences of two verbs such as these, juxtaposed within a single clause with no conjunction or complementizer, are known as Serial Verb Constructions. I will refer to the type of construction illustrated above in Hmong as the 'Attainment Serial Verb Construction'.

The way in which the attainment of goal is expressed in the English version of (1') is different in one respect from the Hmong example, but similar to it in another. While English does not introduce a second verb, as in the Hmong counterpart with <u>tau</u> 'get', it does utilise the same verb, simply in a different form — <u>sewed</u> rather than <u>sew</u> — to convey the idea that the goal has been attained.

In the English version of (2'), on the other hand, the attainment of the goal is expressed in a totally different way. Rather than repeating, in a different form, the same verb (<u>search</u>) that is used to describe the goal-oriented process, an entirely different verb (<u>find</u>) is introduced to describe the attainment of the goal.[2]

Types of Process: Activities and Accomplishments

In order to understand more about these very different ways of expressing attainment of goal in these two languages, it will be helpful to introduce a well-known distinction between types of processes: the distinction between *atelic* and *telic* processes: 'Activities' and 'Accomplishments' (Vendler 1967, Dowty 1979). Here are some examples of each of these process types.

(3)   'Activities' (atelic): *laugh, run, watch TV, drive a car, search for a ring*
        'Accomplishments' (telic): *run a mile, write a letter, mould a rice cake, sew a skirt*

Activities, such as 'laugh', 'run', 'watch TV', 'drive a car', and so on, describe processes that occur over a period of time and which do not involve any change or result occurring as an inherent part of that process. Theoretically one could go on 'running' or 'driving a car' for any length of time. Although extrinsic factors, such as exhaustion or the end of the road, might cause one to 'stop' at some point, there is nothing intrinsic to the actions of 'running' or 'driving a car' themselves that leads to them inevitably being 'finished'.

Accomplishments, such as 'run a mile', 'write a letter', or 'mould a rice cake', on the other hand, have both a process component and a result component. If you persevere for long enough with the *process* of 'writing a letter' or 'moulding a rice cake', you will ultimately achieve the *result* of having 'written a letter' or 'moulded the rice cake'. Because they involve these two components — a process and its inherent result — Accomplishments have sometimes been characterised as a kind of amalgam of an Activity and a result (for example, Jacobsen 1992: 162).[3]

Although Accomplishments are quite often characterised in this way — as an Activity that leads up to a result — it is important to recognise that the process component of an Activity differs from that of an Accomplishment in a fundamental way. While an Activity involves a homogeneous process — one that is basically the same at its beginning and its end — an Accomplishment involves a non-homogeneous process — one that moves towards the attainment of its own, inherent goal.

The difference between these two types of event is not, however, as this may seem to imply, that Accomplishments have a goal and Activities do not. Instead, Accomplishments differ from Activities in that they have an *intrinsic* goal. A goal of this kind is often appropriately referred to as a 'result' or a 'terminal point'. Accomplishments are 'telic': they are 'directed toward attaining a goal or limit at which the action exhausts itself and passes into something else' (Andersson 1972).[4] In other words, you just can't keep on 'moulding the same rice cake' or 'sewing the same skirt' forever.

Activities may or may not have a goal. You do not have a goal when you 'laugh', for example, but you do when you 'search for your ring'. If Activities do have a goal, however, it must be an *extrinsic* one, because Activities are 'atelic'. Take the Activites 'search for your ring' and 'chase the kids', for example, both of which have clear, but extrinsic, goals:

(5)   a.   search for your ring
        b.   chase the kids

You can persevere for an indefinite period of time 'searching for your ring' or 'chasing the kids' but in the end you may have done no more than that; you may never actually attain your goal of 'finding your ring' or 'catching up with kids'. A goal of this kind is something quite separate from the action described, rather than being a natural 'result' or 'terminal point' of that action. It thus differs in a fundamental way from the intrinsic, telic goal of an Accomplishment.

Attainment of Goal in Activities and Accomplishments

Returning, then, to our original discussion concerning the ways in which the attainment of the goal of a process is expressed in Hmong and in English, we can now use this distinction between Activities and Accomplishments to characterise the differences we have observed.

In English, the attainment of the intrinsic goal of an Accomplishment, such as <u>sew a skirt</u>, is expressed by simply using the same predicate in a different form. Either a past form (<u>sewed a skirt</u>) or a perfect form (<u>has sewn a skirt</u>) will suffice to convey that the process of 'sewing a skirt' has been carried through to its natural terminal point, the creation of a new skirt.

The attainment of the extrinsic goal of a goal-oriented Activity, such as <u>search for a ring</u>, on the other hand, cannot possibly be expressed by simply using the same predicate in English. Neither the past form (<u>searched for a ring</u>) nor the perfect form (<u>has searched for a ring</u>) can serve to convey that the goal has been attained, because the attainment of that goal is not an intrinsic part of the meaning of the predicate. In order to convey the attainment of the goal, it is necessary to employ an entirely different verb (<u>find</u>) in English.

In Hmong, the difference between the intrinsic goal of an Accomplishment and the extrinsic goal of a goal-oriented Activity does *not* result in a difference in the way that the attainment of these goals is expressed. Both the goal of the Accomplishment <u>xaws daim tiab no</u> 'sew this skirt' and that of the Activity <u>nrhiav kuv nti plhaib</u> 'search for my ring', is expressed as attained by the use of a

Serial Verb Construction, involving the addition of a second verb
after the first one: the verb tau 'get' (see examples (1') and (2')).

It is important to note that, although the verb tau 'get' is by
far the most common result verb used in series with another verb
to express the attainment of a goal in Hmong, it is by no means
the only one. A variety of verbs can appear in this role, depending
on the nature of the goal that is attained. This is illustrated in
Examples (6) and (7).

(6)   a. Nws   mus   raws   lawv.
          3SG   go   pursue   3PL
          '*She chased them.*'

       b. Nws   mus   raws   cuag   lawv.
          3SG   go   pursue   reach   3PL
          '*She caught up with them.*'

(7)   a. Lawv   mus   tom   khw   lawm.
          3PL   go   over.there   market PERF
          '*They have gone off to market.*'

       b. Lawv   mus   txog   tom   khw   lawm.
          3PL   go   arrive   over.there market   PERF
          '*They have arrived at the market.*'

In Example (6), the verb raws 'pursue', in the goal-oriented
Activity predicate raws lawv 'pursue them', is followed by the result
verb cuag 'reach' to indicate that the extrinsic goal of this Activity
is attained. In (7), the verb mus 'go', in the Accomplishment
predicate mus tom khw 'go to market' is followed by the result
verb txog 'arrive' to indicate that the intrinsic goal of this
Accomplishment is attained.

More about Accomplishments in Hmong

A question that naturally arises, when we look at Hmong examples
involving Accomplishment predicates, is: 'why do we need the
second verb at all to express attainment of the goal?' Surely, if a
goal-oriented process is telic, and as such is 'directed toward
attaining a goal or limit at which the action exhausts itself and

passes into something else' (Andersson 1972), then simply expressing that process in the past or perfect form will be sufficient to indicate that the goal has been attained.

There seems, however, to be a subtle difference between Accomplishment predicates in Hmong and their equivalents in English. A predicate like <u>xaws daig tiab no</u> 'sew this skirt' or <u>puab</u> <u>ib lub ncuav</u> 'mould a rice cake' seems to involve a greater degree of focus on the process component of the event than its English counterpart, and less focus on the inherent end point.

Thus, in Hmong it is very natural to say, for example:

(8) Nws xaws daig tiab no lawm, tseem tsis tau tag.

    3SG sew CLF skirt this PERF still NEG PFCV finish

    *'*She has sewn this skirt, (but) hasn't finished it yet.'*

(9) Kuv puab ib lub ncuav lawm, tseem tsis tau tag.

    1SG mould one CLF skirt PERF still NEG PFCV finish

    *'*I have moulded a rice cake, (but) haven't finished it yet.'*

The English translations in the examples above are marked with an asterisk, because they sound so odd. When one hears 'She has sewn this skirt' in English, one would take it to mean 'She has finished sewing this skirt'. Likewise, 'I have moulded a rice cake' indicates 'I have finished moulding the rice cake'. The Hmong sentences, on the other hand, are not odd or contradictory in any way, even with perfect or past tense reference. This is because the focus of an Accomplishment predicate in Hmong, like <u>xaws daig</u> <u>tiab no</u> 'sew this skirt', is on the process leading up to the goal, rather than on the goal itself.[5] Dahl (1981: 81ff) notes that Slavic aspectologists observe not one but two distinctions in relation to telicity. He gives the examples listed in (10) to illustrate:

(10)   a.   I was writing.

        b.   I was writing a letter. ('T property')

        c.   I wrote a letter (taken to imply 'I finished it'). ('T property' & 'P property')

The first distinction is between predicates that do not lead up to a terminal point ((10a) above) and those that do ((10b) and (10c)). Dahl coins the term 'T property' to refer to those predicates that do lead up to a terminal point ((10b) and (10c)). The second distinction is between predicates that simply lead up to a terminal point ((10b)), and those for which the terminal point is actually reached ((10c)). This latter property Dahl terms the 'P property' ((10c)).

It seems from examples like (8) and (9) above that Accomplishment predicates in Hmong have the 'T property' but not necessarily the 'P property'. That is, even when they occur in the past or perfect form (as in Example (8) xaws daig tiab no lawm 'sew CLF skirt this PERFECT"), they express an action that leads up to a terminal point, but for which the terminal point has not necessarily been reached. It is interesting to note that Accomplishment predicates in some other Asian-area languages, for example Mandarin and Japanese, exhibit the same kind of properties with regard to telicity (Smith 1990, Jarkey, 1998).

Because these predicates describe actions that lead up to an intrinsic goal (the 'T property'), they are, in the absence of any explicit denial of the achievement of that goal, often taken to imply that the goal *is*, in fact, attained. Observe the following examples:

(11)   Nws   xaws   daig   tiab   no   rau   kuv   lawm.
       3SG   sew   CLF   skirt   this   for   1SG   PERF
       '*She has sewn this skirt for me.*'

(12)   Thaum   yus   puab   ib   lub   ncuav…
       when   INDEF   mould   one   CLF   rice.cake
       '*When one moulds a rice cake…*'

(13)   Niaj   hnub   cov   me nyuam   mus   nram   pas dej.
       every day   CLF.PL   child   go   down   pond
       '*Every day the children go down to the pond.*'

In all three sentences above an Accomplishment predicate is used without any 'support' from an Attainment Serial Verb Construction, and yet there is a clear implication that the goal in each case is attained.[6]

As Smith (1990: 323) points out with regard to similar predicates in Mandarin, however, this implication of the attainment of the goal is simply part of the pragmatic interpretation of predicates like these in many contexts. 'Because telic events involve completion, they may be used to implicate completion.' However, the fact that this implication can be denied or negated in other contexts, shown earlier in Examples (8) and (9), indicates that completion is not part of the *semantic* content of the predicates themselves. Following Comrie (1976: 112), we can say that these predicates are unmarked for the feature of attainment of goal, meaning that they 'simply [say] nothing about its presence or absence'.

The fact that an Accomplishment predicate in Hmong like xaws ib daig tiab 'sew a skirt', by itself, has the 'T Property' but not necessarily the 'P Property' means, then, that it can be used with an implication that the goal is attained. Nevertheless, when these predicates are used, the focus of attention is not on the terminal point at all, but rather on the goal-oriented process. An Attainment Serial Verb Construction xaws tau (ib daig tiab) 'make (a skirt)', on the other hand, unambiguously exhibits the 'P Property'. This means that, although the process leading up to the terminal point is referred to (by the first verb), the focus in this construction is very clearly on the fact that the terminal point (indicated by the second verb) is reached.

This difference in focus is responsible for the tendency for Accomplishment predicates in Hmong to be expressed with a single verb when reporting actions, and with a Serial Construction when reporting results. Compare examples (14) a. and b.

(14) a. Xyoo no   nws   <u>ua</u>   ob   daig   teb.
         year this 3SG   do   two   CLF   field
         '*This year he's working two fields.*'

      b. Xyoo no   nws   <u>ua</u> <u>tau</u> ob   txhab   nplej.
         year this 3SG   do   get   two   platform rice
         '*This year he grew two platforms(-worth) of rice.*'

In (14a), the simple predicate ua ob daig teb (do two fields) appears in a context in which the focus of interest is on the activity of the farmer: 'This year he's working two fields'. In (14b), however, the use of the Attainment Serial Verb Construction ua tau ob nthab nplej (do get two CLF rice) is clearly appropriate. In this case, the focus is not on the activity of the farmer throughout the year, but on the result of that activity at the end of the year: on the product of his or her labour.

Because the Attainment Serial Verb Construction focuses explicitly on the attainment of goal, it would be completely nonsensical and contradictory to follow these sentences with a denial like the ones in Examples (8) and (9) earlier.

(15) *Nws <u>xaws</u> <u>tau</u> daig tiab   no   lawm, tseem tsis   tau   tag.

3SG   sew   get   CLF skirt this   PERF still   NEG get   finish

*'*She has sewn this skirt, (but) hasn't finished it yet.*'

What Might These Differences Mean?

The discussion above has revealed that, when it comes to the expression of attainment of goal, English requires just one verb, while Hmong prefers two. This generalisation applies not only when the predicate involves an intrinsic goal (telic, Accomplishment predicates such as <u>xaws ib daig tiab</u> 'sew a skirt'), but also when it involves and extrinsic goal (atelic, Activity predicates such as <u>nrhiav kuv nti nplhaib</u> 'search for my ring').

The discussion has also revealed that there is a subtle difference between an Accomplishment predicate in English and its nearest equivalent in Hmong. While the past or perfect form of an Accomplishment predicate in English is automatically interpreted as expressing the attainment of its inherent goal ('P Property'), this is not necessarily the case in Hmong. An Accomplishment predicate in Hmong needs the support of a second verb (in an Attainment Serial Verb Construction) in order to unambiguously express attainment of goal.

Differences such as these between two languages might be taken to suggest differences between the ways in which speakers of those languages conceive of the notion of 'attainment of goal'. The fact that simple Accomplishment predicates are unmarked for the feature of attainment of goal in another Asian-area languages — Japanese — has led some linguists to propose this as evidence for a difference in world-view between speakers of this language and speakers of English.[7]

The fact that Accomplishment predicates are unmarked for the feature of attainment of goal in Japanese, Hmong and some other Asian languages *does not* suggest to me that speakers of these languages do not perceive such a goal in basically the same way as speakers of English do: as a specific and unambiguously attainable point. Nor does this seem to me to constitute good evidence for the notion that speakers of these languages view the world in any way differently from speakers of English.

What this lack of markedness in Accomplishment predicates *does* suggest to me is that this feature is not part of the semantic content of the simple predicates concerned. It is the entire clause and not just the simple verb or predicate, of course, that is the domain of the proposition. In these languages, something beyond a simple predicate is required to express a proposition involving this particular semantic concept.

If we look beyond the simple predicate but yet within the clause in Hmong (and in other Asian-area languages such as Japanese and Mandarin) it is immediately apparent that the expression of telic events in which the goal is unambiguously attained — the expression of telic events with the 'P property' in Dahl's terms — is indeed thoroughly alive and well. As shown above, one way in which this is achieved in Hmong is through the use of a Serial Verb Construction involving the support of a result verb appearing in the same clause. Likewise, in other languages of the area, a range of highly productive and frequently occurring multi-verb constructions are prominent among strategies that are used for unambiguously expressing the attainment of the goal of a telic action (Jarkey 1998).

It is important to note that multi-verb constructions in all of these languages have other important functions beyond the aspectual function that is the focus of this chapter. Serial Verb Constructions are used in Hmong to express direction and deixis, cause and effect, and so on (see Jarkey 1991). Furthermore, the Hmong Serial Verb Construction described in this chapter is used not only to express attainment of goal, but also to express ability (Jarkey 1991: 227–31).

Regardless of its other functions, however, this construction is used extremely commonly with the aspectual function described above: to assert the attainment of both the intrinsic goal expressed by an Accomplishment predicate and the extrinsic goal of a goal-oriented Activity predicate. These multi-verb constructions in Hmong express both a goal-oriented process and the attainment of its goal, not within a simple predicate, but nevertheless within a single clause, and thus within a single proposition.

Conclusion

The data presented in this chapter do not support the idea that speakers of Hmong might view the goal of a process in any way differently from speakers of English. While this notion is, indeed, not expressed in a simple predicate with a single verb in Hmong, it is expressed through other means — notably through the use of the Serial Verb Construction described in this chapter.

The clause, rather than the simple predicate, is the domain for the expression of the proposition. If we find incongruence at the level of the predicate between English and Hmong, this may not itself constitute good evidence for assuming differences in cultural perceptions and world-views between speakers of these two languages. It may, instead, simply be evidence for differences in the ways in which the semantic load is distributed in the clause in languages with very different typological characteristics. In this case, at least, we can confidently affirm the sentiments of my friend and teacher Cua: at first glance we may look very different but, underneath, we're all the same!

Footnotes

[1] A different, though perhaps related morpheme, tau, occurs preverbally in White Hmong, and is even more likely to be assumed to signal past tense. The function of this morpheme is actually to mark perfective aspect — to indicate that an event is completed, or will be completed, at the time referred to (see Jarkey 1991: 76–7). In fact there is no morpheme in Hmong that has the simple function of marking past tense.

[2] There are some sets of minimal pairs in English, in which a verb with a prepositional object indicates a goal-oriented action, and the corresponding verb with a direct object indicates the related result: for example, 'shoot at a monkey' versus 'shoot a monkey'; 'kick at someone' versus 'kick someone'. In Swedish, the distinction is more systematic (Dahl 1981:87), for example, stickade på en tröya 'knitted at a jumper' versus stickade en tröya 'knitted a jumper'. In some non-Germanic European languages (for example, Russian, Ancient Greek), a similar distinction is made morphologically, by employing different aspectual forms of the same verb.

[3] Jacobsen uses Vendler's terminology 'Achievement' (Vendler 1967) rather than the word 'result'. Jacobsen attributes this characterisation of Accomplishments to personal communication from James McCawley (Jacobsen 1992: 253, fn 61).

[4] This translation from the original German is from Dahl (1981).

[5] Perhaps better translations might be: 'She has been sewing this skirt …' and 'I have been moulding this rice cake'. It is important to note, however, that there is no explicit marker of imperfective aspect in these Hmong sentences. Imperfective aspect is overtly indicated in White Hmong either by reduplication of the verb, or by the use of an adverb such as tab tom 'have just begun to', tseem 'still', pheej 'continually', sij 'repeatedly', and so on (Jarkey 1991: 75).

[6] The types of contexts in which this implication tends to be reinforced share the feature of 'boundedness' (Dahl 1981, Hopper and Thompson 1980: 285–6).

[7] The highly respected Japanese linguist, Yoshihiko Ikegami, for example, argues that this supports his contention that the English language has a tendency toward a precise, 'individuum' schema, and the Japanese language toward a vague, 'continuum' schema (Ikegami 1981, 1993). He suggests that Japanese tends to be 'oriented toward blurred articulation and a focus on the whole configuration or gestalt and on the continuum' (1993: 813) as opposed to the clearer articulation and focus on the 'individuum' of English.

References

Abadie, Maurice (1924), *Les Races du Haut-Tonkin de Phong-Tho à Lang Son*, Paris: Société d'Editions Géographiques, Maritimes et Coloniales.

Adams, Monni (1974), 'Dress and Design in Highland Southeast Asia: The Hmong (Miao) and the Yao', *Textile Museum Journal*, 4(1): 51–66.

Adler, Shelley R. (1995), 'Refugee Stress and Folk Belief: Hmong Sudden Deaths', *Social Science and Medicine*, 40(12): 1623–9.

Agnew, R. Gordon (1939), 'The Music of the Ch'uan Miao', *Journal of the West China Border Research Society*, 11: 9–22.

Anderson, Benedict (1983), *Imagined Communities: Reflections on the Origins and Spread of Nationalism*, London: Verso.

Anderson, June (1996), *Mayko's Story: A Hmong Textile Artist in California*, San Francisco, CA: California Academy of Sciences.

Andersson, Sven-Gunnar (1972), *Aktionalität im Deutschen: Eine Untersuchung unter Vergleich mit dem Russischen Aspektsystem*, Uppsala: Acta Universitatis Uppsaliensis. Stockholm: Almqvist & Wiksell (distr).

Ang, Ien (1993), 'The Differential Politics of Chineseness', in Ghassan Hage and Lesley Johnson (eds), *Identity, Community, Change*, Kingswood, NSW: Research Centre in Intercommunal Studies, Faculty of Humanities and Social Sciences.

——— (2000), 'Asians in Australia: A Contradiction in Terms?', in John Docker and Gerhard Fischer (eds), *Race, Colour and Identity in Australia and New Zealand*, Sydney: University of New South Wales Press.

Appadurai, Arjun (1990), 'Disjuncture and Difference in the Global Cultural Economy', *Public Culture*, 2: 1–24.

Bays, Sharon Arlene (1994), Cultural Politics and Identity Formation in a San Joaquin Valley Hmong Community, PhD dissertation, Los Angeles, CA: Department of Anthropology, University of California. UMI Order Number 9513829.

Beauclair, Inez de (1960), 'A Miao Tribe of Southeast Kweichow and Its Cultural Configuration', *Bulletin of the Institute of Ethnology, Academica Sinica*, 10: 127–99.

Becker, Carol S. (1992), *Living and Relating: An Introduction to Phenomenology*, Newbury Park, CA: Sage.

Bernatzik, Hugo A. (1947), *Ahka und Meau: Probleme der Angewandten Völkerkunde in Hinterindien*, Inssbruck: Wagner'sche Univ. Buchdruckerei.

———— (1970), *Akha and Miao: Problems of Applied Ethnography in Farther India*, translated from the 1947 German edition by Alois Nagler, New Haven, CT: Human Relations Area Files.

Bessac, Susan L. (1988), 'Embroidered Hmong Story Cloths', Missoula, MT: University of Montana *Contributions to Anthropology*, no. 9, Department of Anthropology.

Betts, George Edgar (1899–1900), 'Social Life of the Miao Tsï', *Journal of the Royal Society*, North China Branch, 33(2): 85–105.

Boilés, Charles L. (1967), 'Tepehua Thought-Song: A Case of Semantic Signalling', *Ethnomusicology*, 11(3): 267–92.

Bolton, Geoffrey (1963), *A Thousand Miles Away: A History of North Queensland to 1920*, Brisbane: Jacaranda Press in association with The Australian National University.

Bottomley, Gillian (1992), *From Another Place: Migration and the Politics of Culture*, Melbourne: Cambridge University Press.

———— (1998), 'Anthropologists and the Rhizomatic Study of Migration', *Australian Journal of Anthropology*, 9(1): 31–44.

Bourotte, B. (1943), 'Mariages et funérailles chez les Mèo Blancs de la région de Nong-Het (Tran Ninh)', Institut Indochinois pour l'Etude de l'Homme, Hanoi, *Bulletin et Travaux*, 6: 33–57.

Brah, Avtah (1996), *Cartographies of Diaspora: Contesting Identities*, London: Routledge.

Bridgman, E. C. (1859), 'Sketches of the Miau-Tsze', *Journal of the Royal Asiatic Society*, North China Branch, 3: 257–86.

Britton, Catherine (1996), 'Learning About "The Curse": An Anthropological Perspective on Experiences of Menstruation', *Women's Studies International Forum*, 19(6): 645–53.

Broumton (1881), 'A Visit to the Miau-Tsze Tribes of South China', *Proceedings of the Royal Geographic Society*, 3: 225–6.

Brown, Katherine (2000), 'Reading Indian Music: The Interpretation of Seventeenth-Century European Travel-Writing in the (re)Construction of Indian Music History', *British Journal of Ethnomusicology*, 9(ii): 1–34.

Bruner, Edward M. (1986), 'Ethnography as Narrative', in Victor W. Turner and Edward M. Bruner (eds), *The Anthroplogy of Experience*, Urbana, IL: University of Illinois Press.

Buckley, Thomas and Alma Gottlieb (1988), ' A Critical Appraisal of Theories of Menstrual Symbolism', in Thomas Buckley and Alma Gottlieb (eds), *Blood Magic: The Anthropology of Menstruation*, Berkeley, CA: University of California Press.

Catlin, Amy (1982), 'Speech Surrogate Systems of the Hmong: From Singing Voices to Talking Reeds', in Bruce T. Downing and Douglas P. Olney (eds), *The Hmong in the West: Observations and Reports*, Minneapolis, MN: University of Minnesota, Southeast Asian Refugee Studies Project.

——— (1997a), 'Puzzling the Text: Thought-Songs, Secret Languages, and Archaic Tones in Hmong Music', *World of Music*, 39(2): 69–81.

——— (1997b), *Hmong Musicians in America: Interactions With Three Generations of Hmong American Musicians, 1978–1996*, Van Nuys, CA: Apsara Media for Intercultural Education. 50 minute videotape.

Cha, Bee (2001), 'Being Hmong is Not Enough', *Paj Ntaub Voice*, 'Silence', 7(2): 8–11.

Chan, Anthony (1990), *Hmong Textile Designs*, Owings Mills, MD: Stemmer House.

Clarke, Samuel R. (1904), 'The Miao and Chungchia Tribes of Kueichow Province', *East of Asia Magazine*, 111: 193–207.

——— (1911), *Among the Tribes in South-West China*, London: China Inland Mission, Morgan and Scott.

Clifford, James (1994), 'Diasporas', *Cultural Anthropology*, 9(3): 302–38.

Cohen, Erik (1989), 'International Politics and the Transformation of Folk Crafts — The Hmong (Meo) of Thailand and Laos,' *Journal of the Siam Society*, 77: 69–82.

———— (1990), 'Hmong (Meo) Commercialized Refugee Art: From
    Ornament to Picture', in Dan Eban, E. Cohen and B.
    Danet (eds), *Art as a Means of Communication in Pre-literate Societies:
    The Proceedings of the Wright International Symposium on
    Primitive and Precolumbian Art*, Jerusalem: The Israel Museum.
Cohen, Robin (1996), 'Diasporas and the Nation-State: From Victims
    to Challengers', *International Affairs*. 72(3): 507–20.
———— (1997) *Global Diasporas: An Introduction*, London: University
    College London Press.
Comrie, Bernard (1976), *Aspect: An Introduction to the Study of Verbal
    Aspect and Related Problems*, Cambridge: Cambridge University
    Press.
Conquergood, Dwight (1992), 'Fabricating Culture: The Textile Art of
    Hmong Refugee Women', in E. C. Fine and J. H. Speer (eds),
    Performance, Culture and Identity, Westport, CT: Praeger
    Publishers.
Craig, Jean (1965), *Refugee Settlers: A Study of Displaced Peoples in
    Australia*, Canberra: Institute of Advanced Studies, Australian
    National University.
Crane, Diana (2002), 'Culture and Globalization: Theoretical Models
    and Emerging Trends', in Diana Crane, Nobuko Kawashima,
    and Ken'ichi Kawasaki (eds), *Global Culture: Media, Arts, Policy
    and Globalization*, London and New York, NY: Routledge.
Dahl, Östen (1981), 'On the Definition of the Telic-Atelic (Bounded-
    Unbounded) Distinction', in Philip J. Tedeschi and Annie Zaenen
    (eds), *Tense and Aspect* (Syntax and Semantics 14), New York, NY:
    Academic Press.
De Lepervanche, Marie (1984), *Indians in a White Australia*, London:
    Allen and Unwin.
Delaney, Carol (1988), 'Mortal Flow: Menstruation in Turkish Village
    Society', in Thomas Buckley and Alma Gottlieb (eds), *Blood
    Magic: The Anthropology of Menstruation*, Berkeley, CA:
    University of California Press.
Diamond, Norma (1993), 'Ethnicity and the State: The Hua Miao of
    Southwest China', in Judith D. Toland (ed.), *Ethnicity and the
    State*, London and New Brunswick, NJ: Transaction Publishers.
———— (1995), 'Defining the Miao. Ming, Qing, and Contemporary
    Views', in Stevan Harrell (ed.), *Cultural Encounters on China's
    Ethnic Frontiers*, London and Seattle, WA: University of
    Washington Press.

Dixon, Robert (1983), *Searching for Aboriginal Languages: Memoirs of a Field Worker*, St Lucia, Qld; New York, NY: University of Queensland Press.

Doktorski, Henry (2000), 'Asian Free-Reed Instruments', Classical Free-Reed Inc. At http://trfn.clpgh.org/free-reed/history/sheng.html. Accessed 11 October 2003.

Donnelly, Nancy D. (1994), *The Changing Lives of Refugee Hmong Women*, London and Seattle, WA: University of Washington Press.

Douglas, Mary (1966), *Purity and Danger: An Analysis of Concepts of Pollution and Taboo*, London: Routledge and Kegan Paul.

Dowty, David R. (1979), *Word Meaning and Montague Grammar: The Semantics of Verbs*, Dordrecht: Reidel.

du Halde, P. (1736), *The General History of China containing a Geographical, Historial, Chronological and Political Description of the Empire of China*, Volume I, London: Printed by John Watts at the Printing Office in Wild-Court near Lincolns-Inn Fields.

Eberhard, Wolfram (1970), 'Marriage Customs and Festivals of the Miaotse of Kueichou', in *Studies in Chinese Folklore and Related Essays*, Wolfram Eberhard, Bloomington, IN: Indiana University Research Center for the Language Sciences; The Hague: Mouton & Co.

Ezzy, Douglas (2002), *Qualitative Analysis: Practice and Innovation*, Sydney: Allen and Unwin.

Fadiman, Anne (1997), *The Spirit Catches You and You Fall Down: A Hmong Child, Her American Doctor, and the Collision of Two Cultures*, New York, NY: Farrer, Strauss and Giroux.

Faderman, Lillian, with Ghia Xiong (1998), *I Begin My Life all Over. The Hmong and the American Immigrant Experience*, Boston, MA: Beacon Press.

Falk, Catherine (1994a), 'The Hmong: Music and Ritual', *Tirra Lirra*, 4(3): 9–13.

———— (1994b), 'Roots and Crowns. The Hmong Funeral Ceremony from Laos to Australia', *Tirra Lirra*, 4(4): 19–24.

———— (1996), 'Upon Meeting the Ancestors: The Hmong Funeral Ritual in Asia and Australia', *Hmong Studies Journal*, 1(1): 1–11.

———— (2003a), 'The Dragon Taught Us: Hmong Stories About the Origin of the Free Reed Pipes *Qeej*', *Journal of Asian Music*, 34(2).

———— (2003b), 'If You Have Good Knowledge, Close It Well Tight:
Concealed and Framed Meaning in the Funeral Music of the
Hmong *Qeej*', *British Journal of Ethnomusicology*, 12(11): 1–33.

———— (forthcoming a), 'Hmong Instructions to the Dead: What the
Qeej says in the *Qeej Tu Siav*, Part 1', *Asian Folklore Studies*,
63(1), 2004.

———— (forthcoming b), 'Hmong Instructions to the Dead: What the
Qeej says in the *Qeej Tu Siav*, Part 2', *Asian Folklore Studies*,
63(2), 2004.

Feld, Steven (1984), 'Sound Structure as Social Structure',
Ethnomusicology, 38(3): 383–409.

Field Bulletin of the China Inland Mission (1948), Western region.

Furth, Charlotte and Ch'en Shu-Yueh (1992), 'Chinese Medicine and
the Anthropology of Menstruation in Contemporary Taiwan',
Medical Anthropology Quarterly, 6(1): 27–48.

Ganguly-Scrase, Ruchira and Roberta Julian (1999), 'Minority Women
and the Experiences of Migration', *Women's Studies International
Forum*, 21(6): 633–48.

Geddes, W. R. (1976), *Migrants of the Mountains: the Cultural Ecology
of the Blue Miao (Hmong Njua) of Thailand*, Oxford: Clarendon
Press.

Gigi Durham, Meenakshi (1999), 'Articulating Adolescent Girls'
Resistance to Patriarchal Discourse in Popular Media', *Women's
Studies in Communication*, 22(2): 210–29.

Goffman, Erving (1959), *The Presentation of Self in Everyday Life*,
London: Penguin.

Good, Mary Jo DelVecchio (1980), 'Of Blood and Babies: The
Relationship of Popular Islamic Physiology to Fertility', *Social
Science and Medicine*, 14B: 147–56.

Gottlieb, Alma (1988), 'Menstrual Cosmology Among the Beng of
Ivory Coast', in Thomas Buckley and Alma Gottlieb (eds),
Blood Magic: The Anthropology of Menstruation, Berkeley, CA:
University of California Press.

Graham, David Crockett (1926), 'Critical Note. The Chian Miao of
West China', *Journal of Religion*, 6(3): 302–7.

———— (1937), 'The Customs of the Ch'uan Miao', *Journal of the West
China Border Research Society*, 9: 13–70.

———— (1954), *Songs and Stories of the Ch'uan Miao*, Washington, DC:
Smithsonian Institution Miscellaneous Collection, Vol. 123, No. 1.

Hage, Ghassan (1998), *White Nation: Fantasies of White Supremacy in a Multicultural Society*, Sydney: Pluto Press.

Hall, Stuart (1976/2002), 'The Television Discourse: Encoding and Decoding', in Denis McQuail (ed.), *McQuail's Reader in Mass Communication Theory*, London: Sage.

———— (1992), 'The Question of Cultural Identity', in Stuart Hall, David Held and Tony McGrew (eds), *Modernity and Its Futures*, Cambridge: Polity Press in association with the Open University.

Heimbach, Ernest (1979), *White Hmong-English Dictionary*, Data Paper No.75, Ithaca, NY: Southeast Asia Program, Cornell University (revised 1979, 1985).

Hein, Jeremy (1994), 'From Migrant to Minority: Hmong Refugees and the Social Construction of Identity in the United States', *Sociological Inquiry*, 64(3): 281–306.

Her, Mymee (1998), 'Hmong Resiliency: Surviving a War and Living a Dream', Keynote address given at the Fourth Annual Hmong National Conference, 'Living the Dream', 16–18 April, Denver, CO.

Higham, Charles (1996), *The Bronze Age of Southeast Asia*, Cambridge: Cambridge University Press.

Hmong Social Cultural Group (2000). See http://www.news2mail.com/soc/culture/hmong.html

Hopper, Paul and Sandra A. Thompson (1980), 'Transitivity in Grammar and Discourse', *Language*, 56: 251–99.

Hosie, Alexander (1897), *Three Years in Western China. A Narrative of Three Journeys in Ssu-ch'uan, Kuei-chow, and Yun-nan*, 2nd edn, London: George Philip and Son.

Hostetler, Laura (1995), Chinese Ethnography in the Eighteenth Century: Miao Albums of Guizhou Province, PhD dissertation, Philadelphia, PA: Asian and Middle Eastern Studies, University of Pennsylvania.

Hudspeth, William H. (1937), *Stone Gateway and the Flowery Miao*, London: The Cargate Press.

Ikegami, Yoshihiko (1981), 'Activity-Accomplishment-Achievement: A Language that Can't Say, "I Burned It, But It Didn't Burn" and One That Can', *Essays in Honor of Rulon S. Wells*, Trier: LAUT Series A87.

———— (1993), 'What Does It Mean for a Language to Have No Singular-Plural Distinction? Noun-Verb Homology and Its

Typological Implication', in Richard A. Geiger and Brygida Rudzka-Ostyn, *Conceptualizations and Mental Processing in Language*, Berlin and New York: Mouton de Gruyter.

Inglis, Christine (1992), *Asians in Australia: The Dynamics of Migration and Settlement*, Singapore: Institute of South-East Asian Studies.

Inhorn, Marcia C. (1996), *Infertility and Patriarchy: The Cultural Politics of Gender and Family Life in Egypt*, Philadelphia, PA: University of Pennsylvania Press.

Ip, D., I. Kawakami, K. Duivenvoorden and L.C. Tye, (1994), *Images of Asians in Multicultural Australia*, Sydney: Multicultural Centre, University of Sydney.

Jacobsen, Wesley M. (1992), *The Transitive Structure of Events in Japanese*, Tokyo: Kuroshio Publishers.

Jarkey, Nerida (1991), Serial Verbs in White Hmong: A Functional Approach, PhD thesis, Sydney: Department of Linguistics, University of Sydney.

———— (1998), 'Expressing Accomplishment in Japanese', Paper presented at the 12th Biennial Conference of the Asian Studies Association of Australia, University of NSW, Sydney.

John Michael Kohler Arts Center (1986), *Hmong Art: Tradition and Change*, Sheboygan, WI: John Michael Kohler Arts Center.

Johnson, Charles R. (ed.) (1985), *Dab Neeg Hmong. Myths, Legends and Folktales from the Hmong of Laos,* Saint Paul, MN: Linguistics Department, Macalester College.

Julian, Roberta (1998), '"I Love Driving!": Alternative Constructions of Hmong Femininity in the West', *Race, Gender and Class*, 5(2): 30–53.

————, Adrian Franklin and Bruce Felmingham (1997), *Home From Home: Refugees in Tasmania*, Canberra: Department of Immigration and Multicultural Affairs.

Koltyk, Jo Ann (1993), 'Telling Narratives Through Home Videos: Hmong Refugees and Self-Documentation of Life in the Old and New Country', *Journal of American Folklore*, 106(422): 435–49.

Kuper, Hilda (1947), *An African Aristocracy: Rank Among the Swazi*, London: Oxford University Press for the International African Institute.

Larsen, Hans Peter (1984), 'The Music of the Lisu of Northern Thailand', *Asian Folklore Studies*, 43: 41–62.

Layne, Linda (1990), 'Motherhood Lost: Cultural Dimensions of
    Miscarriage and Stillbirth in America', *Women & Health*, 16
    (3/4): 69–98.
Lee, Gary Y. (1986), 'Culture and Adaptation: Hmong Refugees in
    Australia', in Glenn L. Hendricks, Bruce T. Downing and Amos
    S. Deinard (eds), *The Hmong in Transition*, New York, NY:
    Center for Migration Studies; Minneapolis, MN: Southeast
    Asian Refugee Studies of the University of Minnesota.
——— (1988), 'The Hmong', in James Jupp (ed.), *Encyclopedia of the
    Australian People*, Sydney: Angus and Robertson.
——— (1996), 'Cultural Identity In Post-Modern Society: Reflections
    on What is a Hmong?', *Hmong Studies Journal*, 1(1): Fall,
    http://members.aol.com/hmongstudiesjrnl/HSJv1n1_LeeFr.ht
    ml (Date last accessed: 9 October 2003).
——— (2001), 'The Hmong', in James Jupp (ed.), *The Australian
    People: An Encyclopaedia of the Nation, Its People, and Their
    Origins*, Cambridge: Cambridge University Press.
Lee, Pa Houa (2002), 'What's New With the Sounders', *Hmong
    American Journal*, 1, April: 36–7.
Leepreecha, Prasit (2001), Kinship and Identity among Hmong of
    Thailand, unpublished PhD thesis, Seattle, WA: University of
    Washington.
Lemoine, J. (1995), 'Les Hmong et les Yao', in Christine Hemmet
    (ed.), *Montagnards du pays d'Indochine dans les collections du
    Musée de l'Homme*, Paris: Editions Sépia.
Lewis, Alison (2000), 'The Western Protestant Missionaries and the
    Miao in Yunnan and Guizhou, Southwest China', in Jean
    Michaud (ed.), *Turbulent Times and Enduring Peoples. Mountain
    Minorities in the South-East Asian Massif*, Richmond, Surrey:
    Curzon Press.
Liamputtong, Pranee (2002), 'Gender, Sexuality and Marriage Among
    Hmong Youth in Australia', in Lenore Manderson and Pranee
    Liamputtong (eds), *Coming of Age in South and Southeast Asia:
    Youth, Courtship and Sexuality*, Surrey: Curzon Press.
Liamputtong Rice, Pranee (1995), 'Pog Laus, Tsis Coj Khaub Ncaws
    Lawm: The Meaning of Menopause in Hmong Women',
    Journal of Reproductive and Infant Psychology, Special Issue on
    The Menopause, 13(2): 79–92.

——— (1998), 'Children! Children!: The Social Construction of
    Infertility Among Hmong Women in Australia', Paper
    presented at the Fourth National Hmong Conference, Denver,
    Colorado, USA, 16–18 April.
——— (2000), *Hmong Women and Reproduction*, Westport, CT:
    Bergin and Garvey.
——— and Douglas Ezzy (1999), *Qualitative Research Methods: A
    Health Focus*, Melbourne: Oxford University Press. 7
Liang, Yuanrong (1987), 'Miao Dances', in Chen Weiye, Ji Lanwei and
    Ma Wei (eds), *Flying Dragon and Dancing Phoenix: An
    Introduction to Selected Chinese Minority Folk Dances*, Beijing:
    New World Press.
Lin, Yueh-Hwa (1940–41), 'The Miao-Man Peoples of Kweichow',
    Harvard Journal of Asiatic Studies, 5: 261–345.
Lipsitz, George (1994), *Dangerous Crossroads: Popular Music,
    Postmodernism and the Poetics of Place*, London and New York,
    NY: Verso.
Liu, Chung Shhe Hsien (1934), 'Sur un instrument musical à anches
    libres en usage chez les Miao dans la Chine du Sud-Ouest',
    L'Ethnographie, 28/29: 27–34.
Liu, Terry (2002), 'Chao Yang's story',
    http://www.actaonline.org/features/sound%20traditions/yang.h
    tm Accessed 12 October 2003.
Lockhart, William (1861), 'On the Miautsze or Aborigines of China',
    Transactions of the Ethnological Society, 10.
Lumholtz, Carl (1889), *Among Cannibals: An Account of Four Years'
    Travels in Australia and of Camp Life with the Aborigines of
    Queensland*, translated by R. B. Anderson, New York, NY: C.
    Scribner.
Lunet de Lajonquière, Émile (1904), *Ethnographie des territoires
    militaires*, Hanoi: Schneider.
——— (1906), *Ethnographie du Tonkin Septentrional*, Hanoi and Paris:
    E. Leroux.
Mareschal, Eric (1976), *La musique des Hmong*, Paris: Musée Guimet.
Martin, Denis-Constant (1995), 'The Choices of Identity', *Social
    Identities*, 1 (1): 5–20.
Martin, Emily (1992), *The Woman in the Body: A Cultural Analysis of
    Reproduction*, Boston, MA: Beacon Press.
Martin, Jean (1978), *The Migrant Presence*, Sydney: Allen and Unwin.

McGilvray, Dennis (1982), 'Sexual Power and Fertility in Sri Lanka: Batticaloa Tamils and Moors', in Carol P. MacCormack (ed.), *Ethnography of Fertility and Birth*, London: Academic Press.

Mercer, Kobena (1988), 'Diaspora Culture and the Dialogic Imagination: The Aesthetics of Black Independent Film in Britain', in Mbye B. Cham and Claire Andradé-Watkins (eds), *Blackframes. Critical Perspectives on Black Independent Cinema*, Cambridge, MA. The MIT Press, pp. 50–61.

Mickey, Margaret Portia (1947), 'The Cowrie Shell Miao of Kweichow', *Papers of the Peabody Museum of American Archaelogy and Ethnology*, XXX11(1): vii–83.

Mingyue, Liang (1985), *Music of the Billion. An Introduction to Chinese Musical Culture*, New York, NY: Heinrichshofen Edition.

Minichiello, Victor, R. Aroni, E. Timewell and L. Alexander (1995), *In-Depth Interviewing: Principles, Techniques, Analysis*, 2nd edn, Melbourne: Longman.

Moua, Mai Neng (2001), '"Silence" in the Hmoob Community', *Paj Ntaub Voice*, 'Silence', 7(2): 4.

Moule, A. C. (1908), 'A List of the Musical and Other Sound-Producing Instruments of the Chinese', *Journal of the North China Branch of the Royal Asiatic Society of Great Britain and Ireland*, 39: 1–161.

Moustakas, Clark (1994), *Phenomenological Research Methods*, Thousand Oaks, CA: Sage.

Naisbitt, John (1995), *Global Paradox*, New York: Avon.

Neuenfeldt, Karl (1997), *The Didjeridu: From Arnhem Land to Internet*, Sydney: John Libbey and Company/Perfect Beat Publications.

Nusit Chindarsi (1976), *The Religion of the Hmong Njua (Blue Miao)*, Bangkok: The Siam Society.

Oakes, Tim (1998), *Tourism and Modernity in China*, London and New York: Routledge.

OMA (Office of Multicultural Affairs) (1989), *National Agenda for a Multicultural Australia: Sharing Our Future*, Canberra: Australian Government Publishing Service.

Pao, Saykao (2002), 'The Root and the Fruit: Hmong Identity in the future'. Unpub. mss. based on keynote speech presented at the 7th Hmong National Conference, Milwaukee, 14–16 April.

Patterson, Carolyn B. (1986), 'In the Far Pacific at the Birth of Nations', *National Geographic*, 170(4): 460–99.

Peterson, Sally (1988), 'Translating Experience and the Reading of a Story Cloth', *Journal of American Folklore*, 101(399): 6–22.

Pfaff, Tim (1995), *Hmong in America: Journey From a Secret War*, Eau Claire, WI: Chippewa Valley Museum Press.

Prendergast, S. (1994), *This is the Time to Grow Up: Girls' Experiences of Menstruation in School*, London: Family Planning Association.

Radano, Ronald and Philip V. Bohlman (2000), 'Music and Race, Their Past, Their Presence', in Ronald Ranaldo and Philip V. Bohlman (eds), *Music and the Racial Imagination*, London and Chicago, IL: University of Chicago Press.

Rex, John (1995), 'Ethnic Identity and the Nation-State: the Political Sociology of Multi-Cultural Societies', *Social Identities*, 1(1): 21–34.

Rosaldo, Michelle Zimbalist (1974), 'Women, Culture and Society: A Theoretical Overview', in Michelle Zimbalist Rosaldo and Louise Lamphere (eds), *Woman, Culture and Society*, Stanford, CA: Stanford University Press.

Rozario, Santi (1992), *Purity and Communal Boundaries: Women and Social Change in a Bangladeshi Village*, London: Zed Books.

Savina, F. M. (1930), *Histoire des Miao*, Hong Kong: Société des Missions Etrangères de Paris.

Schein, Louisa (1989), 'The Dynamics of Cultural Revival Among the Miao in Guizhou', in Chien Chiao and Nicholas Tapp (eds), *Ethnicity and Ethnic Groups in China*, Hong Kong: New Asia Academic Bulletin, Chinese University of Hong Kong.

——— (1996), 'Multiple Alterities: The Contouring of Gender in Miao and Chinese Nationalism', in B. Williams (ed.), *Women out of Place*, London and New York, NY: Routledge.

——— (1999), 'Diaspora Politics, Homeland Erotics, and the Materializing of Memory', *Positions*, 7(3): 697–729.

——— (2000), *Minority Rules: The Miao and the Feminine in China's Cultural Politics*, London and Durham, NC: Duke University Press.

Schotter, P. Aloys (1909), 'Notes Ethnographiques sur les Tribus du Kouy-tcheou (Chine)', *Anthropos*, 4(1): 318–53.

Schutz, A. (1974), 'The Stranger', in Brigitte Berger (comp.), *Readings in Sociology: A Biographical Approach*, New York, NY: Basic Books.

Schwörer-Kohl, Gretel (1981) 'Sprachgebundene Mundelorgelmusik zum Totenritual der Hmong in Nordthailand und Laos', Bayreuth: Bericht über den Internationalen Musikwissenschaftlichen Kongress.

——— (1982), 'Uber den Begriff *Ntiv* in der Musikterminologie der Hmong in Nordthailand und Laos', *Jahrbuch fur Musikalische Volks-und-Volkerkunde.*

Scott, George M. (1986), Migrants Without Mountains. The Politics of Sociocultural Adjustment Among the Lao Hmong Refugees in San Diego, PhD dissertation, SanDiego, CA: University of California at San Diego.

Seidenfaden, Erik (1923), 'The White Meo', *Journal of the Siam Society,* 17 (3): 153–89. Translation of the work by Luang Boriphandh Dhuraratsadorn.

Shi Jing (Book of Odes) (1998) http://etext.lib.virginia.edu/chinese. Accessed 11 October 2003.

Smith, Carlota S. (1990), 'Event Types in Mandarin', *Linguistics,* 28: 309–36.

Sobo, E. J. (1992), '"Unclean Deeds": Menstrual Taboos and Binding "Ties" in Rural Jamaica', in M. Nichter (ed.), *Anthropological Approaches to the Study of Ethnomedicine,* Amsterdam: Gordon and Breach Science Publishers.

Spivak, Gayatri Chakravorty (1990), *The Post-Colonial Critic: Interviews, Strategies, Dialogues,* edited by Sarah Harasym, London: Routledge.

Sreberny-Mohammadi, Annabelle (1991), 'The Global and the Local in International Communications', in James Curran and Michael Gurevitch (eds), *Mass Media and Society,* London: Edward Arnold.

Stern, Theodore (1976), 'Drum and Whistle "Languages": An Analysis of Speech Surrogates', in Thomas A. Sebeok and Donna Umiker Sebeok (eds), *Speech Surrogates,* The Hague: Mouton.

Symonds, Patricia V. (1991), Cosmology and the Cycle of Life: Hmong Views of Birth, Death and Gender in a Mountain Village in Northern Thailand, PhD dissertation, Providence, RI: Anthropology, Brown University.

——— (1996), 'Journey to the Land of Light: Birth Among Hmong Women', in Pranee Liamputtong Rice and Lenore Manderson (eds), *Maternity and Reproductive Health in Asian Societies,* Amsterdam: Harwood Academic Press.

———— (2003), *Calling in the Soul: Gender and the Cycle of Life in a Hmong Village*, London and Seattle, WA: University of Washington Press.

Tapp, Nicholas (1989), *Sovereignty and Rebellion: The White Hmong of North Thailand*, Singapore: Oxford University Press.

———— (2000), 'Ritual Relations and Identity: Hmong and Others', in A. Turton (ed.), *Civility and Savagery: Social Identity in Tai States*, Richmond, Surrey: Curzon Press.

———— (2001), *The Hmong in China: Context, Agency and the Imaginary*, Leiden: Brill.

———— (2003), 'Exiles and Reunions: Nostalgia Among Overseas Hmong (Miao)', in Charles Stafford (ed.), *Living with Separation in China: Anthropological Accounts*, London and New York, NY: RoutledgeCurzon.

———— Jean Michaud, Christian Culas, and Gary Lee (eds) (forthcoming), *Hmong/Miao in Asia*, Chiangmai: Silkworm Books.

Thomas, Mandy (1999), *Dreams in the Shadows: Vietnamese–Australian Lives in Transition*, Sydney: Allen and Unwin.

Thuren, Britt-Marie (1994), 'Opening Doors and Getting Rid of Shame: Experiences of First Menstruation in Valencia, Spain', *Women's Studies International Forum*, 17(2/3): 217–28.

Urry, John (2002), *The Tourist Gaze*, London: Sage.

Vang, Maykou Margaret (1994) Hmong Mothers and Daughters: Cultural Adjustment and Conflict, MA thesis in Interdisciplinary Studies, Cultural Anthropology, California State University, Stanislaus.

Vendler, Zeno (1967), *Linguistics in Philosophy*, Ithaca, NY: Cornell University Press.

Wang, Jennifer (1998–99), 'The Hmong Community in Sydney: Demography, Education and Employment, Pre- and Post-Arrival', *Lao Studies Review*, 3.

Werbner, Pnina (1996), 'The Fusion of Identities: Political Passion and the Poetics of Cultural Performance among British Pakistanis', in David Parkin, Lionel Caplan and Humphrey Fisher (eds), *The Politics of Cultural Performance*, Oxford: Bergahn Books.

———— (1998), 'Diasporic Political Imaginaries: A Sphere of Freedom or a Sphere of Illusions?', *Communal/Plural*, 6(1): 11–31.

Wu, Charles L. (1940), 'Glimpses of the Miao Tribes in Kweichow',
     China Quarterly, 5: 837–43.
Wu, Xiaoping (2000), 'Ethnic Tourism — A Helicopter From "Huge
     Graveyard" to Paradise? Social Impacts of Ethnic Tourism on
     the Minority Communities in Guizhou Province, Southwest
     China', *Hmong Studies Journal*, 3: 1–20.
Xiong, Nao (1999), 'The Hmong Khaene'. At
     http://www.cauchico.edu/-cheinz/syllabi/asstoo1/spring99/
     xiong_n/myasst1.htm Accessed 15 August 2002.
Xiong, Tou Ger (1998), *Hmong Means Free*, Video produced by Tou
     Ger Xiong.
Yang, Dara Carol (2002), 'Single … Longer', *Hnub Tshiab*, 3(1): 1–2.
Yang, Mu (1993), *Chinese Musical Instruments*, Canberra: Coralie
     Rockwell Foundation, Australian National University.
Yang, Naly (2001), 'I walk a fine line', *Paj Ntaub Voice*, 'Silence', 7(2):
     46.

Notes on Contributors

Dr Catherine Falk is the Head of Ethnomusicology as well as the Deputy Dean in the Faculty of Music at the University of Melbourne. Her early research concerned the village music of West Java; for the last twelve years she has been working on the text and music of the Hmong funeral ritual with Hmong people in Australia. Some of the recent results of her research will appear in *The Journal of Asian Music, Asian Folklore Studies* and the *British Journal of Ethnomusicology* in 2004.

Dr Nerida Jarkey received her PhD in Linguistics from the University of Sydney in 1991 for her research on the syntax and semantics of White Hmong. She taught English and Linguistics at the University of Uppsala (Sweden) before becoming a lecturer in Japanese Studies at the University of Sydney in 1995. In 2003 she was appointed Director of First Year Teaching and Learning in the Faculty of Arts at the University of Sydney. Her current research interests cover: the semantics of grammar in Japanese, Hmong, and other Asian languages; language style and metaphor in Japanese women's magazines; and the learning experience of first year undergraduate students.

Dr Roberta Julian is Associate Professor and Director of the Tasmanian Institute of Law Enforcement Studies at the University of Tasmania. She is a sociologist who has published widely in the areas of immigrant and refugee settlement, ethnicity and health, globalisation and diaspora, and the relationships between class, gender and ethnic identity. Her most recent publication is

Australian Sociology: A Changing Society (Pearson Longman, 2003) which she co-authored with David Holmes and Kate Hughes. She has been researching Hmong for over ten years and has published book chapters and journal articles on Hmong identity and Hmong women in *Race, Gender and Class, Asian and Pacific Migration Journal* and *Women's Studies International Forum*.

Dr Gary Yia Lee, a former Colombo Plan student from Laos, completed a first degree in Social Work from the University of New South Wales, and was the first Hmong to complete a PhD in Anthropology, from the University of Sydney in 1981. He has taught at Sydney University and Macquarie University and was recently Visiting Fellow at The Australian National University. He has written many articles on the Hmong refugees and their cultural traditions which have been put on his own website (http://www.atrax.net.au/userdir/yeulee/index.htm) for the benefit of young Hmong readers and other researchers, and recently retired as Senior Ethnic Liaison Officer for the Ethnic Affairs Commission of the State of New South Wales.

Dr Pranee Liamputting is an Associate Professor at the School of Public Health, La Trobe University, Melbourne. She has researched and published extensively on cultural and social influences on immigrant women's reproductive and sexual health and other health-related issues in Australia. Her recent publications include *Hmong Women and Reproduction* (Bergin and Garvey, 2000), and (co-edited with Lenore Manderson) *Coming of Age in South and Southeast Asia: Youth, Courtship and Sexuality* (Curzon, 2002).

Dr Nicholas Tapp is Senior Fellow in the Department of Anthropology at The Australian National University. Previously he lectured at Edinburgh University, and at the Chinese University of Hong Kong. He has researched on the Hmong in China and Thailand, with briefer research visits to Vietnam and Laos, and his books include *Sovereignty and Rebellion : the White Hmong of Northern Thailand* (Oxford University Press, 1989), and *The Hmong of China : Context, Agency, and the Imaginary* (Brill, 2001).

Dr Maria Wronska-Friend is a Polish anthropologist and museum curator specialising in Southeast Asian textiles. In 1987 she received a PhD from the Institute of Arts of the Polish Academy of Sciences in Warsaw for her research on Javanese batik. In 1992 she moved to Australia, taking the position of lecturer at the Material Culture Unit (currently the School of Anthropology and Archaeology) at James Cook University in Townsville, north Queensland. In 1995–97 she was Curator of the touring exhibition 'Migrants from the Mountains' on Hmong textile arts; she has conducted fieldwork in Indonesia, Papua New Guinea and among Hmong and Polish immigrants in Australia.

Index